Listen to God Daily

Lily L. Loh

Published by Aventine Press
55 East Emerson St.
Chula Vista CA 91911
www.aventinepress.com

ISBN: 978-1-59330-833-9

Printed in the United States of America

DEDICATION

To

my loving Father
in heaven

To

Jesus Christ
my spouse

To

the Holy Spirit
who inspires me

FOREWORD

By Fr. John H. Hampsch, C.M.F.

Often the yearning for something sweet can be quickly satisfied by a single piece of soft candy, like fudge. But sometimes one might prefer a lingering sweetness, and choose a slowly-dissolving piece of hard candy.

Our sacred Catholic liturgy is bespangled with countless scriptural gems of revelation that communicate to us uplifting insights sometimes called "divine love-whispers." Some of them provide the soul with a momentary but satisfying spiritual uplift, the way that fudge immediately satisfies the "sweet-tooth" craving. Other liturgical passages from God's word provide thought-provoking insights that draw us into a more sustained grace-flavored and love-savored "hard candy" form of extended wonderment.

This little treatise is an unpretentious but well-supplied "candy store," well stocked with both kinds of sweets by its compiler, Lily Loh, who has attached her own insights to scriptural excerpts from the Eucharistic liturgy. Readers who take time to relish this "collection of confections" will soon experience the transforming power of God's word in their lives.

Fr. John H. Hampsch, C.M.F.

Author of Healing Your Family Tree

FOREWORD

By Rev. Msgr. Richard F. Duncanson

"Listen to God Daily" is a delightful invitation to discover how God speaks to us each day through the readings at Mass. The Second Vatican Council reminded us that when the Scriptures are read at Mass, it is truly Jesus Christ himself who is speaking to us. But do we really listen? Journaling helps us not only to listen to Jesus, but to recall and reflect on what He is telling us. Lily Loh's method is one that can work for each and every one of us. Reading her book will certainly encourage us to give it a try."

Rev. Msgr. Richard F. Duncanson

Pastor of Mission Basilica San Diego de Alcala

ACKNOWLEDGMENTS

My special thanks to Pauline Wright who encouraged me to start journaling and writing a few years ago. She taught me how to listen to the Holy Spirit. Ever since that time, I have been journaling every day.

My gratitude to Angie Lake who has taught me so much at the Women's Christian Fellowship Bible Study. She has inspired me to meditate and to write down God's visions and revelations after reading Scripture.

I am forever grateful to my good friends who have helped me with my manuscript, Jackie Eginton, Kathryn and Dan Kremer and Thor Strom. They have spent many hours making corrections and suggestions. Thanks to Judy O'Connor who did an excellent job in designing the book cover for me. My friends Kitty Morse and Carole Bloom, who have written many books, gave me much helpful advice and encouragement.

Without the healing prayer ministers who have prayed over me and encouraged me, this book would never have been written. Their love and support for me are priceless. I especially want to thank Helena Kim, Dr. Janice Nadler, Cory Graves, Kathy Lawson, Mary Ann Schuyler and many other friends in the healing ministry.

Many thanks to my family, especially my mother-in-law, Grace Loh, my daughter, Christina Loh, and my son, Derek

Loh for their encouragement and support. Special gratitude to my sister, Helen Tsou, and my brother, Thomas Lee, whose faith and love for God are examples for me to follow.

Last, but not the least, I want to thank God the Father for the Holy Bible which contains the living words for my daily meditation. Thank you, Jesus, for your words of wisdom. Without the Holy Spirit, this book would never have become a reality.

INTRODUCTION

How would you like to have a friend who calls you up and starts talking and talking non-stop? When he or she finishes talking, they hang up and never give you a chance to answer them back. This is the way many people talk to God. We seldom bother to listen to what God wants to say to us in answer to our prayer. Jesus calls us to be his friends. Yet, many of us never know how to listen to him.

Several years ago Pauline Wright, our music director and healing prayer minister, prayed over me during one of our healing services at St. James Church. She told me she saw a pen above my head and that God was calling me to start journaling. Since that day, I read the Bible readings for daily Mass each morning and listen to what I feel God is revealing to me through the Scripture. I then write my reflections in my journal.

During that same time, I was participating in Women's Christian Bible Study Fellowship at St. Elizabeth Seton Church led by Angie Lake. Every week we had homework. At the end of each page we had to write our meditations and revelation. This exercise helped me to learn how to listen to God in a deeper way.

At the beginning my journal page was filled with my own thoughts and very few words from God. By the second year, I was able to listen to God more and more. Gradually I stopped writing my own reflections and the entire page became what God was telling me through words or visions. Many people are often surprised when I tell them that I am journaling what God is speaking to me. Jesus said, "I am with you until the end of time." (Matthew 28:20) He is talking to each one of us all day long. Are we listening? We are so busy and distracted by the world around us. It is not easy to be totally quiet in order to hear the voice of the Lord.

In the Bible, many verses invite us to listen to God. "Listen to my voice; then I will be your God and you shall be my people." (Jeremiah 7:23) "O that today you would listen to his voice." (Psalm 95:7) At the Transfiguration, God said to the three disciples, Peter, James and John, "This is my beloved son in whom I am well pleased – listen to him!" (Matthew 17:5) How can we put that into practice ourselves?

For me, mornings are the best time to meditate and listen to God because this is my quietest time of the day. I usually wake up around 6 AM. The first thing I do is read the daily Scriptures of the Mass at least twice. Then I pick a sentence that speaks to me. I choose a word or two for my meditation that day. Next, I sit quietly and ask the Holy Spirit **to open me to receive God's Word.** Usually after a few minutes of total silence, I hear God speaking to me in my spirit. I write God's words in red ink. Any of my own responses or questions to God are written in a different color ink. This way when I re-read journal entries at any time, I know the red words are those I felt God gave me that particular day. His words are like a two edged sword. They are powerful.

When I re-read my old journals the words of God still speak to me in a very meaningful way.

Here are a few suggestions to help you start journaling:

1. To get into the listening mood, find a quiet place where you can journal without any interruption.
2. Sit upright, breathing slowly and deeply a few times.
3. Relax and feel the presence of God.
4. Invite the Holy Spirit to guide you and enlighten you.
5. Read the Scriptures for the day or any passage from the Bible slowly and let the words speak to you. Read attentively twice, **noticing how these words affect you**.
6. Close your eyes and be still. Focus on Jesus or God the Father or the message in that Scripture.
7. Pick up your pen. Date your page, and write your first name as if God is dictating a letter directly to you. Then, write whatever comes into your mind. Do not worry about misspelling or grammar.
8. After writing, thank God for what has been revealed to you and re-read all you have written.

At first, you might have only a few words or a sentence. Do not get discouraged. Gradually you will be able to write a page or two. You probably have heard "a picture is worth a thousand words". Sometimes God will give you a vision or scene in your mind instead of words. Since I am a very visual person, God often speaks to me in this form.

How do you know that these writings, visions and teachings are from God? First of all, what you receive from God never contradicts the Bible because the Word of the Lord is truth. God **wants** to reveal the truth to us. Secondly, there is no condemnation from our loving God who is always here to affirm us and teach us, even when we are being corrected. Jesus said that he came not to condemn but to save. He wants to build an intimate relationship with us, letting us know how much he loves us. Thirdly, you will be glad that you took this half hour to spend alone with Our Lord and you will see in time that it bears good fruit. I am quite sure you will be surprised by the grace of Our Lord's merciful love.

By writing this book, I hope to inspire others to listen to God through the practice of daily journaling which has helped me tremendously for the last several years. By spending this time alone with the Lord each morning, I now feel closer to God and realize so much more that God truly loves me. Also, by meditating on the Scriptures, Mass has become so meaningful to me. Throughout the day I am aware of God's presence. In many ways I hear and experience the Lord speaking to me.

I hope this book will encourage ***you*** to start journaling. Just as God has blessed my quiet time, so shall you surely be blessed! May the Holy Spirit guide you and fill you with wisdom and joy!

Blessings and prayers,

Lily L. Loh

Listen to God Daily

AN HEIR

January 1

"So you are no longer a slave but a child, and if a child then also an heir, through God." Galatians 4:7

In my vision I saw God our Father standing in front of Jesus who was surrounded by all those who love him. Jesus brought us to his Father and introduced us to him as his brothers and sisters. God said to me, "My precious child, everyone who acknowledges my Son will be saved. You are now my child and will inherit everything that I have planned for you. You will enjoy eternal life and peace beyond your understanding. You will be surrounded by love in heaven. You will be called my chosen one. Every time you call me 'Abba', I will answer you for I have made you my heir. So rejoice and be glad. It is a day of celebration!"

Lord, I thank you for adopting me as your child. I am overjoyed to be a part of your holy family, Father, Son and Holy Spirit.

STAR

January 2

"We saw his star at its rising and have come to do him homage." Matthew 2:2

My precious child, when you are at the lowest point of your life that is when I reveal myself to you. I come to those who are simple, needy and totally dependent on me. The wise will be able to find me in the world and in my word. I am always there like a star to guide you. All you need to do is to look towards heaven. Let go of all your earthly desires. Be observant like the shepherds and the magi. You will see me and find me, for I will reveal myself to all those who seek me. I come as a newborn babe, totally unpretentious and loving.

My Jesus, I long to hold you in my arms. I love you with all my heart. Guide me to the right path.

SPIRIT OF GOD

January 3

"This is how you can know the Spirit of God: every spirit that acknowledges Jesus Christ come in the flesh belongs to God, and every spirit that does not acknowledge Jesus does not belong to God." 1 John 4:2-3

Do not be deceived by the world, my child. Only my Son, Jesus, is the true God. He will lead you to me. He is the way, the truth and the life. Whoever believes in him will have the Holy Spirit. Invoke the name of Jesus often and he will fill you with love and peace beyond your understanding. His name has power to overcome all evil. When you pray in his name, he will do all that you ask him. Do not be afraid to call on him. He loves to hear your prayers. He will answer you always. Like a good shepherd, he will come to rescue you whenever you need him. He will carry you to safety. He will always be there for you.

Jesus, I trust in you. I know your spirit is truth. You are the Son of God.

BEGOTTEN BY GOD

January 4

"Beloved, let us love one another, because love is of God; everyone who loves is begotten by God and knows God."
1 John 4:7

My precious child, you are begotten by God. You are made into our image and likeness. You are our beloved child, for you were conceived in your mother's womb with love. You grew up surrounded by your loving family. You were nurtured and pampered by everyone. All the love that you have received is from me for I love you with an everlasting love. Now go and spread this love to all your family and friends, especially those who are less fortunate than you are. You have been richly endowed. Now go and share what you have with others. Let the example of Elizabeth Seton be your guide. She too was a mother and later started the Sisters of Charity. Go and spread my love to others.

Loving Father, thank you for all your love. Thank you, Jesus, for dying on the cross for me. Thank you, Holy Spirit, for coming into my heart.

LAMB OF GOD

January 5

"Behold, the Lamb of God, who takes away the sin of the world." John 1:29

In my vision I saw a little lamb ready to be slaughtered, cooked and eaten. Jesus said to me, "My loving child, I was killed so that you might live. I laid down my life for you so that you might have my flesh to eat and my blood to drink. Without me, you will not have life in you. With me you will have abundant life. A life filled with love and laughter. A life filled with meaning and purpose. A life filled with my joy. You will feel peaceful and rewarded. You will feel accomplished because you will be filled with my Spirit. He will guide you and protect you from all harm. He will lead you on the right path. He will give you strength to endure all hardship for my sake. You are my loving child and nothing will separate us. I love you."

Lord Jesus, I thank you for coming into this world to save me. I love you with my whole heart.

FOOD

January 6

"'Give them some food yourselves.' But they said to him, 'Are we to buy two hundred days' wages worth of food and give it to them to eat?'" Mark 6:37

My dearest child, I never ask you to give more than you can afford. All I ask from you is to share with those in need with what you have. I can multiply a few fish and bread that my disciples had and feed them to 5,000 men. Whatever you share with others, you will always have enough for yourself. You can trust in me. My disciples had twelve baskets of leftovers. Each disciple received more than he gave away. Do you understand me now? It is more blessed to give than to receive. Give generously to all who ask from you. Your reward will be great in heaven.

Give me a generous heart like yours, Jesus. Help me always to be ready to share with others what you have given me.

MURDERER

January 7

"Everyone who hates his brother is a murderer, and you know that no murderer has eternal life remaining in him." 1 John 3:15

Hatred kills; love gives life. Always choose to forgive and to love. Let no hatred get into your heart. Fill your heart with compassion and mercy. Hatred is from the evil one. It is like poison that kills the soul. Choose life, love and joy. I came into this world not to condemn but to love. Receive my love and your love for others will increase. I am your bottomless well of love.

Lord, give me more of your love so that I may love all those who do not love me in return.

IGNORANCE OF GOD

January 8

"All men were by nature foolish who were in ignorance of God, and who from the good things seen did not succeed in knowing him who is." Wisdom 13:1

In my vision I saw a bellboy delivering a large box to a lady. She was so elated with the present that she never asked who it was from. Jesus said to me, "My child, this is how the foolish people in this world are. They admire the nature and the beauty of the world that I have created, but never acknowledge the creator. Only the wise know that everything comes from my Father who loves to lavish good things to his children. But you, my child, you know him and you love him more than anything here on earth. He is the giver of all goodness that surrounds you. Everything you have comes from him. Love him and cherish him above all. One day you will see him face to face and you will be awestruck by his beauty and his love for you."

My God and my Lord! You are my creator and my all. There is no one like you.

IN SPLENDOR

January 9

"Rise up in splendor! Your light has come, the glory of the Lord shines upon you." Isaiah 60:1

My precious child, in order for you to receive my light you need to repent and confess your sins daily. Be cleansed and be spotless so that my light can shine through you onto others. I am well pleased with you, my child, especially when you empty yourself and listen to my voice. You have purged your own agenda and made room for all those who are in need of my love. Go and be my light.

Lord, may your light shine through me onto others. My soul magnifies my Lord and my Savior.

LOVE AND BLESS

January 10

"He will love and bless and multiply you; he will bless the fruit of your womb." Deuteronomy 7:13

When my disciples came to send the crowd away, I told them to give them food themselves. So likewise, I want you to give love and blessing to everyone and I will multiply your love and blessings ten-fold. But, first you have to give them whatever you have. I can only do miracles when you cooperate with me and trust in me. I want to bless and provide for you all your needs. Even your children and your grandchildren will be blessed because of you.

Open my heart and my hands, Lord. Let me be as compassionate and generous to all as you are.

ANGELS

January 11

"Let all the angels of God worship him." Hebrews 1:6

My angels surround me wherever I go. They were there the day I was born. They announced to the shepherds in the field about my birth. They were there when I suffered in the garden praying alone. My disciples were too tired to pray with me. They were all asleep. But my angels ministered to me and gave me encouragement. Your angels were also there for you when you were born. They have guided you throughout your life, especially in times of your need. They love you and they protect you. They will bring you closer to me. They will guide you on the right path. They are there to serve me and to serve you. They are created for you and for me.

My guardian angel, be with me today. Guide me to Jesus' heart. Let me never be separated from him.

SEVEN OTHER SPIRITS

January 12

"Then it goes and brings back with itself seven other spirits more evil than itself, and they move in and dwell there; and the last condition of that person is worse than the first." Matthew 12-45

My precious, there are good spirits and evil spirits. The good spirits are spirits of love, compassion, mercy, kindness, gentleness and patience. The evil spirits are spirits of greed, hatred, jealousy, pride, anger, lust and sloth. Fill yourself with the Holy Spirit and there will not be any room for the evil spirits to move into your soul. Keep your eyes fixed on me and follow me closely. Never waver from your goal to please me. Only in this way will you keep the evil one out. Keep the commandments and be good. Let nothing distract you from me. Make room only for me. With me you will have nothing to fear.

Come, Lord Jesus. Come and dwell in my heart. Let me never be separated from you. Let me be one with you.

BAPTISM

January 13

"Jesus came from Galilee to John at the Jordan to be baptized by him." Matthew 3:13

My precious child, do not worry about your children. They are my children too. I want them to have the Holy Spirit as much as you do. But they must submit themselves to God first, as I did at the river Jordan. Then God, my Father, will shower them with the Holy Spirit. Continue to pray for them daily. Do not give up. All will happen at the proper time.

Thank you, God, for loving me and my family. I know you have the best future in mind for all my loved ones. Lord Jesus, I trust in you!

GLORIOUS CROWN

January 14

"You shall be a glorious crown in the hand of the Lord, a royal diadem held by your God." Isaiah 62: 3

You are my delight. I enjoy holding you in my hands. Like a lily – you are pure and true. I love to look at your inner beauty. You know how to love. You are obedient. You are precious in my eyes. I love you more than your children love you. I love having you as my bride. I will be with you always and will guide you in all you do. I care about every detail of your life. You are mine.

Lord, I am yours. I give you my heart and my all. Keep me always close to your heart. Let me feel your love forever.

RISING VERY EARLY

January 15

"Rising very early before dawn, he left and went off to a deserted place, where he prayed." Mark 1:35

In my vision I saw myself sitting next to Jesus in a deserted place. The two of us watched the sun slowly rising. It filled the sky with a beautiful golden glow. It was at this moment we both knew that God was with us. Jesus said to me, "My precious child, it is in the silence that you will hear me speaking to your heart. When you are sitting quietly next to me, you will realize the greatness of my Father's love for you. You are the apple of his eye. He will shield you from all harm. He will protect you all the days of your life if you stay close to him. Only sin can separate you from us. Come away with me to a deserted place often. Enjoy the beauty surrounding you. Only then will you discover who you really are."

My Jesus, open my eyes to see you everywhere I go. Teach me how to pray. Open my ears and my heart so that I can hear you better.

WILL IT

January 16

"Moved with pity, he stretched out his hand, touched him, and said to him, 'I do will it. Be made clean!'" Mark 1: 41

My precious child, yes, it is my will that everyone will be healed and saved. But you have to come to me and ask for this. You must repent and turn to me in all your ways. Otherwise the healing will not be effective. The root of many illnesses is sin – the sins of others and your own sins. So the first step is to repent and to accept my will for you. After being healed, spread the good news to all who want to hear. Tell them how you were healed. Bring others to me, so that I may heal them too.

Thank you, Lord, for healing my tuberculoses, ulcer, cancer, arthritis, and many other illnesses. You are truly my healer and my redeemer.

SINNERS

January 17

"I did not come to call the righteous but the sinners." Mark 2:17

My precious child, I came to call sinners because they realize that they need me, which is the first step. Without me, you can do nothing. With me, all things are possible. A repentant sinner has compassion and forgiveness for others, for he has received mercy and forgiveness from me. It is impossible to love others if one has never been loved. The righteous think that they have it all, while the repentant sinners are clinging on to me and seeking my love.

Lord, I am a sinner and I need your forgiveness and mercy. Be with me always.

LISTENING

January 18

"Speak, Lord, for your servant is listening." 1 Samuel 3:9

Anytime you ask me a question, I will answer you. So, do not be afraid to ask. I am always there for you. Ask me for directions and I will show you the way. Ask me for my guidance and I will lead you there. Ask me for all your needs and I will provide for you. Ask me for the fruits of the Spirit and you shall have them. So be eager to listen to me and you will hear my voice.

Here I am Lord. I am listening. Speak to me. Send your Holy Spirit upon me and I shall be renewed.

MOUNTAIN

January 19

"He went up the mountain and summoned those whom he wanted and they came to him." Mark 3:13

In my vision I saw myself walking up a mountain with Jesus at my side. It was hard work, but I realized that the less I carried (my worries and my sin) the easier the climb. The only thing I needed during the climb was water – Jesus' living water – which is His grace. Jesus is the way – he guides me. Jesus is my light – he shows me the path. Jesus protects me with his staff and rod. He upholds me.

Lord Jesus, thank you for calling me to go up the mountain with you. You called me and I followed you. Without you I could not have made it to the top.

LORD OF SABBATH

January 20

"That is why the Son of Man is Lord even of the Sabbath."
Mark 2: 28

My precious child, come to me always and rest in me. Sabbath is a day set aside to spend quiet time with me so I can refresh you and renew you. When you are with me, you have nothing to fear. I will bathe you in my living water. You will feel rejuvenated and ready to serve and do my will. That is why it is important to keep the Sabbath holy. For without spending time with me you can do nothing. You need to be recharged every day by my grace. I am your strength and your life. So come and rest in me.

Lord, thank you for giving us a day to rest on the Sabbath, which is a holy day to spend with you. You are my Lord and my God.

HARDNESS OF HEART

January 21

"He looked at them in anger and grieved at their hardness of heart." Mark 3: 5

My child, I was angered and grieved with the Pharisees because they had no love for me or for others. They were only concerned with following the law, not the love of people. I am a God of love. You will never grieve me if you put love above all else. Every time you love, you act like my children. As a child of God, you will inherit eternal life with me in heaven. So harden not your heart. But have love, mercy and compassion towards one another. Imitate me.

Lord, give me more or your love and your compassion so that I will be able to love others as you love me.

WISDOM

January 22

"She opens her mouth in wisdom and on her tongue is kindly counsel." Proverb 31:26

My precious child, learn from Mary, my mother. She was always loving and spoke wisely. Learn to ponder more and speak less. Every word spoken will be played back at you when you die. So speak with prudence. Words have power. They can heal or hurt. Always speak with love and blessings for others.

Mary my mother, pray for me. Help me to speak blessings to others and to bring joy to their souls.

NEW WINE

January 23

"New wine is poured into fresh wineskins." Mark 2:22

The new wine is the Holy Spirit. It was poured into people like my disciples and my mother, Mary. They were open and receptive. They were ready to change and to expand. They were flexible and willing to go out to proclaim my good news to others. They were always growing with the Holy Spirit. They are perfect models for you to imitate, my child. If you want to drink this new wine, you must have a new attitude towards life and towards others. My wine will bring joy to your heart. You will see things and everyone with new eyes. It will surprise you how different your outlook on life will be. It is almost like living in paradise. For my wine will give you energy to carry out the things I want you to do for me. It will invigorate you and strengthen you. You will feel light-headed with joy. So ask for the new wine.

Lord Jesus, you are my joy and my life. In you I find true happiness. Please fill me with your Holy Spirit.

LIGHT

January 24

"I will make you a light to the nations, so that my salvation may reach to the ends of the earth." Isaiah 49: 6

My precious child, always have oil in your lamp. Without oil there will be no light. The oil is the Holy Spirit and my grace. Read the Bible; pray constantly and stay close to me. Only in this way will you be in tune with me and the Holy Spirit. Without us you have no light to guide others to God. Without me you can do nothing. Be my light and be my love.

Lord, give me more of your oil. This way my light will never go out and others will be guided towards you.

PROCLAIM THE GOSPEL

January 25

"Go into the whole world and proclaim the gospel to every creature." Mark 16: 15

My child, the more quiet time you spend with me, the more courage you will have to proclaim my gospel to all. I will give you the insight and the word of knowledge on how to approach others in a way that they will listen to you. Always ask me first before you approach anyone how you are to proclaim the gospel to them. Only in this way will it be effective.

Loving Father, give me the courage and the boldness to speak the good news to everyone who comes into my life.

RECEIVE MERCY

January 26

"So let us confidently approach the throne of grace to receive mercy and to find grace for timely help." Hebrews 4:16

You always forgive your family when they hurt you. Do you think that I will not do the same for you? Because you are my precious child, I love you more than anyone in your family and friends. I will always forgive you. My heart aches whenever you have sinned against me. It is for that reason that I suffered and died on the cross. Come to me and I will wash you clean. I will heal you all your selfishness and lack of compassion for others. I will change your heart and give you a new heart. I will restore you to the person I have created you to be, for you are precious to me. I love you.

Lord, have mercy on me. Christ, have mercy. I am not worthy for all you have done for me. I am a sinner.

REPENT

January 27

"Repent, for the kingdom of heaven is at hand." Matthew 4:17

My dear child, if you only knew the seriousness of sin, you would avoid it like a plague. Sin turns you slowly away from me. And before you know it, you have your back facing me. Every time you sin, it is like throwing mud at me and hitting my face like the soldiers did. So repent always. Only through repentance will you be able to change. Without repentance, you will continue to sin and walk away from me.

I am heartily sorry for having offended you, my Lord. Please give me the grace to sin no more.

DO YOUR WILL

January 28

"Behold, I come to do your will, O God." Hebrew 10: 7

My precious child, first you need to abandon your own will before you can do mine. Then, you need to follow me and carry your cross. Be not afraid to suffer because of me, but rejoice and be glad, for your reward will be great. By doing my will, you are helping me to build my kingdom. Do not waste one day without asking me first what I want you to do for the day. You are my hands and my feet.

Here I am, Lord. I come to do your will. Give me the courage to always say "yes" to you.

RICH SOIL

January 29

"Those sown on rich soil are the ones who hear the word and accept it and bear fruit thirty, sixty and a hundredfold." Mark 4: 20

Keep your soil moist at all times with my living water. Without water, nothing can grow. Weed often. Let not the evil one rob your nutrients from your soil. Cultivate your soil to soften it, so that you will be receptive, compassionate, humble and understanding. Bear not only fruit but flowers too.

Lord, enrich my soil so that I will be able to bear much fruit for your honor and glory. Let me always be ready to blossom and to flower for you.

FAITH

January 30

"Faith is the realization of what is hoped for and evidence of things not seen." Hebrews 11:1

Do you yet not know that with me all things are possible? I have power over everything, even the wind and the storm. The disciples were terrified and thought that they were going to be drowned in the storm. They had me in the boat with them and were still worried and anxious. My child, when you realize that I live within you, you will never have fear or worry. I am in control and no evil will come upon you.

My Jesus, please increase my faith so that I will be able to trust you totally. Let me always feel your presence within me.

THE MEASURE

January 31

"The measure with which you measure will be measured out to you, and still more will be given to you." Mark 4:25

In my vision I saw myself wearing an apron which I held by two corners so that Jesus could pour the seeds from his big round tray into my apron. As soon as I finished spreading the seed, he gave me more. It was so joyful, almost like playing a game, full of laughter and joy. Jesus said to me, "My faithful servant, it is indeed a joy to spread my word to others. The more you give, the more you will receive, for my words have power. They will change lives. It is like a two-edged sword. It will set the captives free and cut them loose from past sins. It will renew them, refresh them and bring them into the abundant life which I have planned for each one. Go now and spread my words to all you meet."

Here I am Lord. I come to do your will. Your word is a lamp to my feet.

HAVE FAITH

February 1

"Why are you terrified? Do you not yet have faith?" Mark 5:40

My precious child, do not be afraid to touch others and pray for their healing, even when they seem to be hopeless. Have faith in me, for I am your God and the author of life. I created everyone on this earth. I can give life even to dry bones. Everything is possible if you have faith. When you have faith in me I will be able to do all miracles. Without faith, I can do nothing. Be not afraid to ask for any kind of healing.

Lord, give me more of your faith. Fill me with your love and compassion.

ANXIETIES

February 2

"I should like you to be free of anxieties." 1 Corinthian 7:32

Have no anxiety whatsoever for I am living in your heart. Would I allow any harm to come to you? Never! Even when you go through fire, you will not be burned. Trust in me. Know that I will rescue you and protect you always. You are never alone. I watch you like the apple of my eye. I hold you in the palms of my hands. Keep focused on me like a sunflower facing towards the sun. You will always be under my watchful eyes.

Lord, remove all anxieties from my soul. Help me to trust you more and more, for you are the center of my life.

BOAST

February 3

"Whoever boasts, should boast in the Lord." 1 Corinthian 1:31

My loving child, I have created you from nothing. When you realize that you are nothing then you are truly being who you are. Everything belongs to me. So do not feel prideful in your accomplishments, for without me, you can do nothing. But with me, you can do all things. Nothing is impossible with me. I am your loving God.

Everything I have comes from you, Lord. Let me never boast about myself, but let every word I speak glorify and praise you. You are my Lord and my God!

DISCIPLINE

February 4

"Endure your trials as 'discipline'; God treats you as sons. For what 'son' is there whom his father does not discipline?" Hebrew 12:7

My child, you have seen one miracle after another. You know how much I love you and want only the best for you. So be at peace and do not worry about anything. Every trial that comes your way will discipline you to be a better and holier person. I love you as my precious child. I will protect you from all harm. I will give you the strength to endure all suffering. Fear not. I am with you always.

Lord, give me peace and endurance to face all my trials. I know how much you care about me. I surrender all to you.

FULL ACCOUNT

February 5

"Prepare a full account of your stewardship." Luke 16:2

My loving child, the way to prepare a full account of your life is to meditate with me each day all your actions, words and thoughts. The moments that you were so happy and loved are the times that you realized how close I was with you. The moments that you were sad and unsure of yourself were the times when you were far from me. Live each day with me in your heart. This way you will never regret any word, action or thought. You will do everything to please me only. For you know I see every detail of your life and always ready to support and uphold you. Every thought that comes to your mind will be inspired by my words and every word you say will glorify me. Live each day as the last day of your life ready to give a full account to me.

Have mercy on me, Lord. I invite you to be with me always. Never let me be separated from you. I only want to live for you.

DEEPLY DISTRESSED

February 6

"The King was deeply distressed, but because of his oaths and the guests he did not wish to break his word to her." Mark 6:26

Every action has consequence. Loving actions will bear much fruit while hurtful actions will harm people. Before you do any action you should always ask me first and wait for my reply. Sometimes it is difficult to embrace the cross. Many people want the easy way out. But to do loving actions requires sacrifice and self denial. Imitate me in all you do. Let my love shine through you to others. This way you will never regret nor be distressed with your actions.

Lord, I want to follow you always. Help me to imitate you daily. Let my actions speak of your love to others.

DESERTED PLACE

February 7

"Come away by yourselves to a deserted place and rest a while." Mark 6:31

My precious child, when you are alone with me in a deserted place that is where I can renew you and refresh you. You can rest in me for my yoke is always easy and my burden light. I will never give you more than you can manage. So come to be alone with me often. I will give you courage to go on. I will give you a new outlook and perspective on each situation. I love to spend quality time alone with you. Even I needed a rest between helping others. It is not possible to give and give without replenishing yourself with my love. You need to be strengthened against the evil one. You must do all things in collaboration with my Father's will. Otherwise all is in vain. So come and rest in me.

Here I am, Lord. Speak to me, comfort me, encourage me and renew me. I am Yours.

PRIDE

February 8

"The beginning of pride is man's stubbornness in withdrawing his heart from his maker; for pride is the reservoir of sin, a source which runs over with vice." Sirah 10:12-13

In my vision I saw a little child stomping her feet and saying, "I can do it by myself!" God said to me, "My child, anyone who thinks that he can be self sufficient and does not need me is like the little girl in your vision. You know in your heart that you cannot do anything without me. It is pride that is the root of all evil. Pride comes before a fall. Pride makes one think that he is better than what he really is. He thinks that he knows it all. This is a sure sign of arrogance and self conceit. But you, my precious child, knows that without me you are nothing. Everything you have belongs to me. I have created you from dust and to dust you shall return for I am your maker and your creator."

Loving Father, I thank you for making me in your image and likeness. You are my creator and my redeemer. I owe you for everything.

HUMAN TRADITION

February 9

"You disregard God's commandment but cling to human tradition." Mark 7: 8

In my vision I saw a beautiful Christmas setting with mistletoe hanging and a beautiful Christmas tree with lights. But the people in it were cold and distant with each other. There was no warmth or love present. Jesus said to me, "Now you understand what it feels like when people just do the traditions without the true meaning of what they are doing. Without love everything you do is like an empty gong. It has no purpose or meaning. Let every action you do be filled with my love for others. Without my love it will not bring others closer to me. It will only bring glory to yourself. With me, you will be able to manifest my transforming love to others. Go and be my heart to others."

Lord, your law of love is more important than any human law. Fill me with your love.

HEARTS

February 10

"These people honor me with their lips, but their hearts are far from me." Mark 7:6

My child, actions speak louder than words. Those people who pray only and do nothing are those who worship me with their lips only. Prayer should always lead to action. Without action, prayer is like empty words. When I created this universe, I spoke the word and the world became a reality. So it is with your prayer. Whatever you pray for, you have to do something about it. Otherwise you are only praying in vain. What I want from you is your heart. Anything done without love is useless. It is self pride.

My joy is to do your will, Lord. I want to love you and honor you with my whole heart.

ONE TRIBE

February 11

"I will leave your son one tribe for the sake of my servant David and of Jerusalem, which I have chosen." 1Kings 11:13

David's heart was always very close to me. He loved me and repented all his sins while Solomon's heart was with his foreign wives and his heart was turned away from me. My child, it is the heart that matters. The first commandment is to love me above all and have no other God besides Me. Many people say that this person will go to heaven because he has been a good person. They forget that the most important commandment is to love me above everything else. And the second commandment is to love your neighbor as yourself.

Lord, you alone are my God. I love you with my whole heart and soul.

DEAF HEAR

February 12

"He makes the deaf hear and the mute speak." Mark 7:37

My love, I am always speaking to you, but you can only hear me when you are silent and listening. Here are the 6 S's: Sit, Still, Silence, Solitude, Simple and Surrender. Do this and you will hear me. Only in silence can you hear my voice. Without silence, the noise of the world will drown out my soft whispering voice. That is why the prophets often go to deserted places to pray so as to be able to hear me. Everyone should be able to hear my voice if they remain quiet and united with me. I will lead you and guide you in all you do. During this Lent try to spend more quiet time alone with me. You will enter a deeper relationship with me. Put out your antenna to receive my messages before you speak. This way you will be my conduit of peace and love for others. When you speak, truth will be revealed to all.

I want to hear your voice, Lord. Open my ears so that I will be able to hear you better. Speak Lord, your servant is listening.

GLORY OF GOD

February 13

"Whether you eat or drink, or whatever you do, do everything for the glory of God." 1 Corinthians 10:31

My beloved, notice how a little child always wants to carry her favorite blanket or doll with her at all times. This is how I would like you to go through each day with me by holding onto me as your most precious possession. Hold on to me as your life depends on me. Do everything with me. Give me the honor and glory in all you have accomplished each day. Never do anything alone and for your own glory. Your life will only have meaning when you are doing my will. When you build your own house alone, it is like building it on sand. Soon the water will wash it away. But when you do things in my honor, it is like a house built on rock. It will stand forever.

I praise you and glorify you, my God and my Lord. In you I trust my whole being.

BE PERFECT

February 14

"So be perfect, just as your heavenly Father is perfect." Matthew 5:48

In my vision I saw a beautiful valentine heart with laces and all the trimmings around it. Jesus said to me, "My love, be as perfect as this beautiful valentine heart. Love each one with a complete love as my Father does. He is such a generous God. When you ask for something he always gives you more than you need. As with the multiplication of loaves and fishes there are always leftover. That is the kind of love that my Father has for you and for everyone. That is perfect love: always giving, always generous, always ready to listen and to love. A perfect love will heal all ills and problems. Give love generously to all the people around you. May your love for others be as perfect as the love my Father has for you."

Lord Jesus, give me your heart. I love you above all people and things. I am yours. Be my Valentine!

HE SIGHED

February 15

"He sighed from the depth of his spirit and said, "Why does this generation seek a sign? Amen, I say to you, no sign will be given to this generation." Mark 8:12

My precious child, people who come to me to see signs and wonders do not love me. They just want to see my power. They do not believe that I am the Son of God and I have all power from my Father. All I need to do is to say the word and it will be done. I came into the world not to show how much power I have but to show how much I love each one of you. Your health and your well being are what I care about most. Do not come to seek signs and wonders but come to seek my love.

My Jesus, it pains me to see you sigh from the depth of your soul. You must be very discouraged with the lack of faith of the Pharisees. All they wanted is signs, not your love for them. Jesus, I love you.

CROWN OF LIFE

February 16

"Blessed is he who perseveres in temptation, for when he has been proved he will receive the crown of life that he promised to those who love him." James 1:12

In this life there will always be temptations. But with my help you will be able to overcome all evil. Temptations are not from me but from Satan. Even I was tempted when I was in the desert for 40 days. He comes especially when we are weak. So keep yourself strong with self discipline and fasting. Stay close to me always and call on me often. Invoke my name whenever you are tempted, for my name has power. It can overcome all evil. I have your crown of life waiting for you in heaven. Keep focused on me and you will finish the race. Come to me, my love.

Lord, be always at my side, for you are my rock and my salvation. Guide me to the right path. Give me the strength to follow you and help me to overcome all temptations.

FASTING AND WEEPING

February 17

"Yet even now, says the Lord, return to me with your whole heart, with fasting, and weeping, and mourning; rend your hearts, not your garments, and return to the Lord, your God." Joel 2:12

My precious child, all I want is your heart. When you turn yourself 100% towards me, it will be the day of rejoicing for me. Fasting will help you to unclutter your life. It will make you more loving and caring to those in need. It will sharpen your awareness of my presence. It will make you more dependent on me for all your needs. Fasting is not only good for your soul, but for your body too. Greed and gluttony are two of the great sins that prevent people from reaching for my love. People are so full of themselves that there is no more room for me. Fast only for me, my love.

Lord, please forgive me for all the times that I have sinned against you. Help me to fast and repent during this Lent. My soul is hungry for your love and presence.

DENY HIMSELF

February 18

"If anyone wishes to come after me, he must deny himself and take up his cross daily and follow me." Luke 9:23

In my vision I saw a baby just learning how to walk. He first took a few tiny steps, wobbly, unsteady and slowly approaching his parent. Jesus said to me, "My loving child, it is the same with your spiritual walk towards me. At first you must take baby steps. Even though you might fall many times, do not worry or be afraid. Just get up and try again. Eventually you will be able to walk towards me and to follow me everywhere I go. You will find joy in following me. You will be able to deny your own will and do my will. I will take you and guide you to where I want you to go. But first you must take a step forward. Keep your eyes upon me and I will give you the strength and the wisdom to follow me."

Call me to come to you, Lord Jesus. I want to follow you wherever you want me to go.

BLIND MAN

February 19

"When they arrived at Bethsaida, they brought to him a blind man and begged Jesus to touch him." Mark 8:22

My precious child, come closer to me and let me touch you, for my touch can heal. When you stay close to me, you will be able to see the spiritual world as I see it. You will know the truth, and the truth will set you free. Bring others to me so that they too might see me and know the truth. The truth will be revealed gradually, like this blind man's eyesight. The more time you spend with me, the clearer you will be able to see me.

Lord, heal my blindness. Let me see you more clearly. I long for the day when I will see you face to face.

RIGHTEOUS

February 20

"I have not come to call the righteous to repentance but sinners." Luke 5:32

In my vision I saw Jesus eating dinner with the Pharisees, the scribes, tax collectors and the twelve disciples. A bright light surrounded Jesus. All the other people were in darkness except the twelve disciples who had little lights above their heads. Jesus said to me, "The reason the disciples have the light is because they have repented from their sins. They realize that they need me. All the other people are in darkness because they do not realize that they are sinners. They think that they are following the law and will be saved. But there is no light of love in their hearts. Because of their judging of others and their complaints they have sinned in God's eyes. They feel that they are superior. Actually, they are full of pride."

Lord Jesus, I confess that I have sinned and I need you in my life. Please remove my pride and self-righteousness. I need your mercy and forgiveness.

TEMPTATION

February 21

"When the devil had finished every temptation, he departed from him for a time." Luke 4:13

My child, when you are being tempted just fix your eyes on me instead of on the devil. Do not try to do anything without me. Use my words from the scripture as I did. You will overcome all temptations when you recite my words. Call on my name which is above all names. At the sound of my name the evil one will flee. You can only serve one master, either me or the evil one. Choose me. I will give you abundant life while the devil only wants to harm you. Have no dealings with him. Every time you are tempted, immediately say my name. Be like a little child calling her mother. Let it be second nature to you. Stay close to me and I will protect you from all harm, for you are mine.

Hold my hand, Lord, so I will not be lost or tempted to follow the evil one. You alone are my God. You alone will I serve.

YOUR SINS

February 22

"It is I who wipe out for my own sake, your offenses; your sins I remember no more." Isaiah 43:25

My precious child, if you only knew how much sins offend me, you would try never to sin again. Sin is like spitting at my face, rejecting me. Sin is turning away from me and separating you from me. I suffered scourging, hitting and being nailed to a tree for all your sins. The wage of sin is death. Avoid all temptations to sin. I have forgiven all your past sins. Start a new day doing good and praising God. The more you love others, the more you will be forgiven.

Lord Jesus, I am heartily sorry for having offended you. Have mercy on me, a sinner. Please help me to avoid future occasions of sin.

KINGDOM OF HEAVEN

February 23

"I will give you the keys to the kingdom of heaven." Matthew 16:19

In my vision I saw myself dressed in white like a bride. There was a beautiful diamond tiara on my head. My dress with a cape seemed to glitter with small white Christmas lights. St. Peter with his keys was standing by the pearly gate of heaven. There on the throne was my bridegroom, Jesus, standing in front welcoming me into his arms. Next to him stood Mary who was dressed in a crystal light blue shining cape. Her smile melted my heart. As I was walking down the aisle, I saw all the people I knew cheering and clapping their hands. I saw many of my friends from church. They were all smiling at me. My heart was so filled with love and joy. It was one of the most beautiful visions that God has given me.

I praise you and I adore you, O Lord! I can hardly wait for the day to be united with you in heaven. St. Peter, please pray for me.

COMMAND

February 24

"Mute and deaf spirit, I command you: come out of him and never enter him again." Mark 9:25

My child, everything is possible with faith and prayer. Ask and you shall receive; knock, it shall be opened to you; seek and you shall find. When you pray for others, have faith that I have heard your prayer and it shall be done. Do not hesitate to ask or have doubt in your heart. Have faith in me. Visualize me raising the dead and healing the sick for nothing is impossible with me at your side. Be bold and step out and have confidence in me. If you command the spirit to come out in my name, it shall be done.

Lord Jesus, everything is possible with you. Increase my faith in you. Help me to trust in you more and more each day.

THE POOR

February 25

"Do not turn your face away from any of the poor, and God's face will not be turned away from you." Tobit 4:7

Whatsoever you do to the least, you do it to me, my child. There are people who are poor materially, some spiritually and some emotionally. The latter are the ones who do not know how to love, for they have not been loved. So go and be my hands and my heart to all those in need. This world is starving for love more than food. This world is moving further away from me. Bring them back to me, my precious child.

Yes, Lord. I will go and minister to the poor for you. Give me more of your love and compassion for all those in need.

SUFFER GREATLY

February 26

"The Son of Man must suffer greatly and be rejected by the elders, the chief priests and the scribes, and be killed and on the third day be raised." Luke 9:22

Love and suffering go hand in hand. Without suffering there is no love. Through suffering you will realize how much I love you. That is why I say, "Pick up your cross and follow me." Through the cross you will turn your life from self love to my love. Your whole attitude about life will be transformed to my will. Every day you will choose to do what is pleasing to me instead of your own pleasures. Suffering leads to new life.

My Jesus, it pains me to know how much you have suffered for me. Loving Father, help me to follow your Son, our Lord and Savior. Never let me be separated from you.

BARREN BUSH

February 27

"He is like a barren bush in the desert that enjoys no change of season, but stands in a lava waste, a salt and empty earth." Jeremiah 17:6

In my vision I saw a barren bush, dry and brittle. When a fire came, it was burned to a crisp in an instant. Jesus said me, "When you are not with me, you will be easily destroyed by the evil one. When you are planted next to me, you will have lush green leaves and bear much fruit, fruit that will last. When the fire comes, you will not perish like the barren bush. So stay close to me. I am the living water. I can put out the fire. No enemy will be able to touch you for you are mine and no harm will come to you. Trust in Me. Hope in Me."

Lord, lead me in your green pasture. You are my living water that refreshes me and renews me.

GLORIFIED BODY

February 28

"He will change our lowly body to conform with his glorified body by the power that enables him also to bring all things into subjection to himself." Philippians 3:21

When you are filled with the Holy Spirit your whole body will be transformed. It will be full of light, radiant like the sun. You will have the warmth of my spirit and my love will permeate your body. It will be transparent, because you will have nothing to hide. Everything will be in the open. There will be no more shame and guilt but instead you will be filled with love, peace and joy. Total contentment! Total surrender to my Father's will. Nothing will prevent you from coming closer to me and to each other. Everyone will be united together with one God and one Savior. Total bliss!

Thank you, Lord, for this vision and understanding of what a glorified body will look like. You are an Awesome God! I can hardly wait for the day that I will have a glorified body like yours in heaven.

CHRIST'S BODY

February 29

"You are Christ's body, and individually part of it." 1 Corinthian 12:27

My precious child, you are in my heart. You are immersed in my love. You are special to me. Go and love others with your generous heart. Never stop giving and sharing. I will give you all the love you need. Remember I have loved you from the moment you were conceived in your mother's womb. You were loved by everyone in your family the day you were born. You are loved by all your friends. Do not be afraid to go and love everyone. It is through your love that I can do miracles for others. It is through your love that I will be able to heal my people. It is through your love that they will know and love me.

Lord, use me. I am yours. Please enlarge my heart so that I will be able to love others as you love me.

FORTY DAYS

March 1

"At once the spirit drove him out into the desert, and he remained in the desert for forty days, tempted by Satan." Mark 1:12

My precious child, it is important to spend time alone with me in silence and away from others. That is when the Holy Spirit will be with you and you will feel my loving presence. It is only through silence that you will be able to hear my voice. During this Lent try to be alone with me more often. You will be changed by my presence. You will overcome all temptations by Satan. With me you will have nothing to fear. You will be bold and will proclaim the good news to everyone you meet.

Lord, help me to be silent as much as possible during these forty days. I want to hear your voice. Fill me with the Holy Spirit.

MY WORD

March 2

"My word shall not return to me void, but shall do my will, achieving the end for which I sent it." Isaiah 55:11

Keep my word in your heart, my love. It will produce fruitful and wonderful results. Be like Mary, my mother. She pondered on my word day and night. My word is a lamp for your feet and a light on your path. Without my word, you will live in darkness. You will be easily led astray. But with my word, miracles and healings will take place, for my word has power and will not return to me empty, but will bring life and joy.

Loving Jesus, your word is my treasure. It is more precious than gold. For it is through your word, the entire universe was created.

TO SERVE

March 3

"The Son of Man did not come to be served but to serve and to give his life as a ransom for many." Matthew 20:28

Unless you serve with a joyful heart, it will not be done with love. Love is the bottom line. A mother is willing to wake up every 2-3 hours to feed her baby. She does it willingly because her love for her baby is great. She will even lay down her life for her child. That is the kind of service I want you to do for others. Imitate me, for I laid down my life for you. I want you to spend eternity with me. Nothing will be too much for me to do for you. You are my precious child. I am willing to die on the cross for you. There is no greater love than to lay down one's life for another. Do likewise.

Lord, give me a servant's heart. Help me not to complain when I have to serve others. I still have a long way to go in loving others the way you have loved me. Help me to be less self-centered and selfish.

THE FASTING

March 4

"This, rather, is the fasting that I wish: releasing those bound unjustly, untying the thongs of the yoke; setting free the oppressed, breaking every yoke; sharing your bread with the hungry, sheltering the oppressed and the homeless; clothing the naked when you see them, and not turning your back on your own." Isaiah 58:6-7

Fasting is not just about food, but about giving your time and your ability to help all those who are in need. It takes time to go and visit the sick and the oppressed. It takes money to buy food for the hungry and clothing for the naked. But most of all, you must bring my love to others who are suffering. Only my love can heal. So during this Lent, be hungry for my love. Seek for my presence whenever and wherever you are. Do good to others. Give up your own agenda and follow my promptings. You will be richly rewarded.

Here I am, Lord. I come to do your will. Help me to be more selfless and generous to all who ask from me.

EVIL GENERATION

March 5

"This generation is an evil generation; it seeks a sign, but no sign will be given it, except the sign of Jonah." Luke 11:29

My precious child, this generation has turned away from me. They are all into themselves. They do things to please themselves instead of God. They do not know what sin is. They have no idea that they have offended me. They have not taught their children about me. They are ignorant of the truth. They worship material goods instead of the One who has created them. They spend their Sundays partying and enjoying their own sports. Their hearts are far away from me. The only way to change is to repent and turn their lives around. There will be no signs except for signs of destruction. Pray for them, my love!

My heart is heavy with guilt, Lord. Please remove all my sins and wash me clean. I want to love and serve you only. Have mercy on me.

THE DOOR

March 6

"Ask and it will be given to you; seek and you will find; knock and the door will be opened to you." Matthew 7:7

The door to my heart is always open for all those who love me. I am like the prodigal son's father, always on the lookout for anyone who has repented of his sins and decided to come home. I will not just open the door, but go running towards him as he walks up to my door. As for you, my love, my door is always open. You can come in and out at any time. My home is your home. You are always welcome. You can come and rest in my heart anytime. I will refresh and renew you. Whenever you need to rest, come home to my heart. My door is never locked. It is the same as when you go to your children's house or your parents' house. Their door is never locked for you. Such is my heart for you.

Lord, I am knocking at your door. Please let me into your precious heart. I love you. I treasure every moment I spend with you alone.

EVERYTHING

March 7

"My son, you are here with me always; everything I have is yours." Luke 15:31

My precious child, you have inherited everything from me so go and use all the gifts that I have given you for the glory of God. Your life will be joyful and fruitful when you realize how richly you are endowed by my loving Father. You will never lack for anything. You will be protected and guided by the holy angels.

Thank you, Lord, for giving me your inheritance which I have not earned. I am in awe of your generosity.

MY HELPER

March 8

"The Lord is my helper, and I will not be afraid. What can anyone do to me?" Hebrews 13:6

I will never leave you nor forsake you, my child. You can count on me. Many of your friends and family say that they will help you. But when you really need them they have one excuse after another. Only I am there always when you call on me. No tears are shed alone. My heart goes out to you when you are in pain and suffering. I will never abandon you. I will be at your side always. You can count on me. For you, I died on the cross and suffered the crucifixion. For you, I endured all the scourging at the pillar and the crowning of thorns. For you, I endured all the spitting and beating. No, I will never leave you. I have paid a price for you. You are my love and my treasure. Just call on me and you will feel my presence. You have nothing to fear. I have sent angels to surround you as you go on your way.

Thank you, Lord Jesus, for your protection and guidance. Thank you for dying on the cross for me. I love you with my whole strength.

I FORGAVE YOU

March 9

"You wicked servant! I forgave you your entire debt because you begged me to. Should you not have had pity on your follow servant, as I had pity on you?" Matthew 18:32-33

Compassion and mercy are who I am. Everyone who wants to follow me must also be compassionate and merciful. I laid down my life to pay for the price of every sin committed. Everyone who loves me will also love others with an unconditional love, without judgment or vengeance. Those who hold unforgiveness in their heart will not be able to love as I do. Their heart is hardened from hatred and resentment. Only those who totally forgive others are set free to love. So, do not hold any grudges or resentment in your heart. Love your enemies.

Lord, give me more of your forgiving love. Help me to forgive everyone in my life who has hurt me in the past. Never let my heart be hardened by hatred or resentment. Fill me with your healing love.

YOUR FAITH

March 10

"'Let it be done for you according to your faith.' And their eyes were opened." Matthew 9:29-30

My loving child, with faith all things are possible. When you have faith in me, you are ready to receive whatever I want to give to you. With faith, you live in the spiritual world. Without faith, you are grounded in this earthly world. The spiritual world has power beyond your imagination. In the spiritual world, your prayers have power to conquer all evil. Faith is to believe in my power. Faith is to know that I am the Almighty God who has created this entire universe. Faith is to know without a doubt that I can change anything with my word. My child, have faith in me. You know how much I love you. Live each day with faith in your heart. You will see miracle after miracle when you live in faith.

Almighty and all loving God, I have faith in you. I know you are the creator and the miracle worker.

LIKE A SPRING

March 11

"He will renew your strength, and you shall be like a watered garden, like a spring whose water never fails." Isaiah 58:11

In my vision I saw a geyser shooting up high in the middle of a fountain. The mist from the water sprayed all around a beautiful garden full of colorful flowers and lush greens. Birds came and bathed in the fountain. Butterflies flew in the air and landed from flower to flower. Jesus said to me, "My child, when you are filled with my love and my Holy Spirit, you are like this beautiful fountain. You will bring joy to everyone around you. You will give hope to those who are in despair. You will speak words of comfort to everyone who needs to hear them. You will strengthen those who are weak. Your soul will be renewed and refreshed like the birds in your vision."

Thank you for this beautiful vision, my precious Jesus. You are the fountain of my life.

LISTEN

March 12

"Listen to my voice; then I will be your God and you shall be my people." Jeremiah 7:23

Whenever you are quiet, my love, you will hear my voice. Whenever you call on me, I will be there for you. Just know that I live in your heart. I know every thought and action you do every day. I am with you always. Talk to me often and listen to my response. I long to communicate with you. I long to spend intimate time alone with you. But if you pack your day with too many earthly activities you will be too busy and distracted to listen to my voice. Did you notice the two memorable times when I spoke to the disciples about my Son? The first time was at his baptism and the second time was at the transfiguration. If you have Jesus in your heart, you will also hear my voice.

Lord, your voice is like honey to my ears. Speak to me Lord; your servant is listening.

FROM YOUR HEART

March 13

"So will my heavenly Father do to you, unless each of you forgives your brother from your heart." Matthew 18:35

My precious child, when you forgive others do not forgive them from your head only but from your heart. There is a difference. When you forgive from your head, you know that you should forgive, but your forgiveness is not complete. When you forgive from your heart, you want only good to happen to others. You want to bless them and wish them well. For I love everyone including sinners. I have forgiven you from all your sins. If I can love you when you were still a sinner, how much more should you not love others and forgive them too? My child, forgive everyone from your heart.

Thank you, Jesus, for forgiving me and saving me from all my sins. Help me never to hold grudges or resentment in my heart. Help me to forgive always.

DEEDS

March 14

"I reward everyone according to his ways, according to the merit of his deeds." Jeremiah 17:10

Deeds speak louder than words. Words sometimes can be empty, but deeds always benefit another person. Do good deeds everyday while you are still capable of doing them. Deeds are good for your soul and you will be rewarded for every good deed you perform each day. Do not let one day go by without doing a good deed for someone. For whatever you do to others, you do to me.

Here I am, Lord. I come to do your will. Let my every deed pleases you.

CORNERSTONE

March 15

"The stone that the builders rejected has become the cornerstone; by the Lord has this been done, and it is wonderful in our eyes." Matthew 21:42

Many people want to build their castles with their own stones and ambitions. Only those who build their lives with me will stand during rain and storm. I am the rock on which everything is created. So build your dreams and desires upon me and you will find true joy and happiness. I am the stone that will carry you through all trials and tribulations. You can lean on me.

Lord Jesus, you are my rock and my salvation. In you, I trust.

CELEBRATE

March 16

"But now we must celebrate and rejoice, because your brother was dead, and has come to life again; he was lost and has been found." Luke 15:32

My precious child, whenever a soul enters into my kingdom there is a celebration with banquets with music and dancing. Each soul is very precious to me. Each soul brings me so much joy, one of the fruit of the Holy Spirit. So be bold in every circumstance to mention my name and to share my story with others. Do not let any chance go by without being a witness for me. There will be celebration and rejoicing for every soul that you bring back to my arms. That is the best gift and sacrifice you can give me.

Lord, I want to bring joy to your heart. Help me to tell others about you and to bring them to you.

NEW HEAVENS

March 17

"Lo, I am about to create new heavens and a new earth; the things of the past shall not be remembered or come to mind." Isaiah 65: 17

In my vision I saw a woman dancing with a tambourine. Everyone around her was rejoicing, singing and dancing. There was so much joy and celebration. Everyone was smiling and laughing. God said to me, "This is the new heaven I am talking about, where there is no hatred or suffering. Everyone is rejoicing for what Jesus has done for each one of you. He came into the world to show you the way, the light and the truth. Whoever believes in him will know the way, the truth and will have the light of life, a life filled with joy and dancing, a life filled with peace and love. So live each day with Jesus in your heart. A new heaven will be waiting for you."

My loving Jesus, I can hardly wait to see you in the new heaven. I want to celebrate and rejoice with you forever.

NEVER FORGET YOU

March 18

"Can a mother forget her infant, be without tenderness for the child of her womb? Even should she forget, I will never forget you." Isaiah 49:15

Yes, I knitted you in your mother's womb. I know every hair on your head. You are precious in my sight. I have formed you into my image and likeness. I died on the cross for you so that you could spend eternity with me in heaven. You are not a mistake but my creation, my pride and my joy. I love everything about you. How could I ever forget you when I have paid the price of saving you with my own blood? No, I will never let you out of my sight. You are the apple of my eye. You are my precious child who will inherit my kingdom. You are chosen by me and my Father. We love you!

Lord, thank you for loving me so much. I feel so blessed to be your beloved child.

JOSEPH

March 19

"The angel of the Lord appeared to Joseph in a dream." Matthew 1:20

My precious child, I have revealed many things to you in your dreams too. I speak to you whenever you are in total silence. When you are asleep you are more open to hear my voice. Joseph was my faithful servant. In his dream, my angel told him about Mary who was pregnant with Jesus. Joseph obeyed and took Mary as his wife. He did what I asked him to do. He was willing to sacrifice his own plans in order to do my will. He even had to leave his own town and spend years hiding in Egypt because of Jesus. You too can do great things for me if you follow my promptings. So be still and know that I am with you always.

Thank you, Lord, for all those wonderful dreams. They have revealed the truth to me. They have brought me closer to you.

OWN RIGHTEOUSNESS

March 20

"Jesus addressed this parable to those who were convinced of their own righteousness and despised everyone else." Luke 18:9

My child, the day that you realize your own imperfections, that is when you are on the road towards perfection. No one is perfect in this world. Only I am perfect. Therefore never think yourself better than others. Everyone has been given special gifts from my Father. Everyone is unique. It is a common sin to think others less righteous than oneself. Repent and change.

Lord, strip me of my pride and self-righteousness. Mea culpa! Mea culpa! Mea maxima culpa!

THE LORD RELENTED

March 21

"So the Lord relented in the punishment he had threatened to inflict on his people." Exodus 32:14

I am always ready to forgive you, my precious child. All you need is to repent for all your sins and to ask for forgiveness. Your intercessory prayers for yourself and for others are brought to my throne by your angels. I hear every one of your prayers. I will relent in punishment when I hear your petitions for I know your heart. You want only to please me. You are often tempted, but you persist in your prayers. You can overcome all evil by prayers. Just say my name "Jesus" and there will be no room for the evil one in your life. My name overcomes all evil. The two cannot coexist together. Choose me always.

Lord, thank you for forgiving me for all my past sins. Your name is like honey to my lips. Jesus, I love you.

BELIEVE IN HIM

March 22

"Just as Moses lifted up the serpent in the desert, so must the Son of Man be lifted up, so that everyone who believes in him may have eternal life." John 3:14-15

The truth is very simple. When Moses lifted up the serpent, all those who looked at it were saved. So it will be for all those who believe in me. They will be saved. With faith everything is possible. When you believe in me, everything will be possible too, for I am your almighty God. I have sent my Son into the world so that you might believe and have eternal life. So believe in him.

Lord, I do believe in you. Help me to trust you more and more.

GALILEE

March 23

"The Messiah will not come from Galilee, will he?" John 7:41

My child, do not put me in a box and confine me to a place. I have created the universe from nothing. I can change the flow of wind and start an earthquake. I am not limited by anything. People on earth are limited and have boundaries. I have none. I can do whatever, wherever I desire. So do not limit me and my ability. The only thing that matters is love, which is not limited or confined. Love expands, grows and can heal all relationships and all ills. Love conquers all. It doesn't matter whether I come from Galilee or Jerusalem. I am God and there is no other. Honor me, believe in me and you shall have abundant life.

My Jesus, I thank you for giving me faith in you. You are all I need. You are my God and my Lord.

DO NOT BELIEVE

March 24

"For if you do not believe that I AM, you will die in your sins." John 8:24

In my vision I saw people standing in the mud. Those who looked up to Christ extended their hands to him and they were lifted up into heaven. Of course they went through a shower of cleansing of all the mud before they were united with Jesus in the kingdom of God. They were purified of their sins. But some people preferred to play in the mud. They were laughing, tugging and pushing people into the mud. They did not want to be saved. They preferred to be in their muddy condition. They were steeped in their sin and did not want to be lifted up by Jesus. I felt so sorry for them.

Lord Jesus, you died on the cross so that we all may be saved. All we need to do is to repent and to believe in your mercy and we will be lifted up to spend eternity with you in heaven. May you be praised and glorified forever.

THE TRUTH

March 25

"If you remain in my word, you will truly be my disciple, and you will know the truth, and the truth will set you free." John 8:31-32

My precious child, every word spoken by me is the truth and has the power to change the world and to change your heart. Ponder my words, read them, chew them and memorize them. My words will give you life and peace in your heart. Those who do not listen or study my words are like little people who are busy doing useless chores, all done in vain. Those who hear me will know the direction they should go and deeds they should do for the honor and glory of my Father. Without my words, there will only be chaos, not peace. With my words, you will have purpose in life. So remember to listen to me at all times, especially early in the morning. This way you will be filled with joy each day.

Speak, Lord; your servant is listening. Your words are more precious to me than gold and silver.

CONSECRATE

March 26

"By this 'will' we have been consecrated through the offering of the body of Jesus Christ once for all." Hebrews 10:10

My loving spouse, you and I are linked together through my body and my blood. A married couple becomes one body. So it is with you and me. See how you did everything to please your husband? You gave up your own will so as to do what he wanted to do. The joy comes when we are together doing my Father's will. For this reason I came into the world. I came to consecrate your life together with mine. Since I have died for your sins you have been redeemed. Come, my beloved, into my kingdom. Have no anxiety and worry whatsoever. I am always by your side. You and I are one. You are mine.

My Lord and my God! I love you more than anyone on earth. For you alone I live each day.

SIGNS AND WONDERS

March 27

"Unless you people see signs and wonders, you will not believe." John 4:48

Some people do not believe until they see signs and wonders. But you, my precious child, believe because you have my love. I will continue to do signs and wonders through you because of your love for others. I cured the official's son because of his love for his son. Love conquers all evil and ills. With love you can change a heart of stone into a heart of flesh. With love all things are possible.

Precious Jesus, I thank you for loving me so much. I believe in your almighty power.

TO STONE JESUS

March 28

"The Jews again picked up rocks to stone Jesus." John 10:31

My precious child, people are afraid of the truth. They are so used to lies that they do not want to hear truth. The truth will set them free. But they would rather live in their own sinfulness. They do not want to change their ways. My child, you know the truth. Do not be afraid to go and tell everyone about me even though they do not want to hear about it. Your duty is to tell them the truth. Whether they accept it or not does not concern you. Plant the seed and let me take care of the rest. The seed will grow when it is nourished and watered. Nothing is wasted when you work for me. All I need is your willingness and your "yes".

Yes Lord, I will go and tell others about you and how great you are. You have the words of everlasting life.

PARADISE

March 29

"Amen, I say to you, today you will be with me in Paradise." Luke 23:43

Anyone who believes in me and loves me will be saved. The criminal who mocked me did not get salvation because of his unbelief. But the criminal who had love and compassion and believed in my power and authority was saved. I came into the world so that everyone might be saved. Salvation is for everyone. My dear child, go out and tell others what I have done for you and your family. Let people know what a loving and saving God they have. I have no arms and feet except yours. So be my hands to heal my people and tell them the good news. I need you to carry on the work that I have started.

Lord, I am ready to do your will. Guide me and lead me along the right path. I look forward to the day when I can join you in Paradise.

COSTLY PERFUMED OIL

March 30

"Mary took a liter of costly, perfumed oil made from genuine aromatic nard and anointed the feet of Jesus and dried them with her hair; the house was filled with the fragrance of the oil." John 12:3

My precious child, every time you love others and do good deeds for others, you express your love for me for I am in every human soul. It is a joy to see all my children loving each other, caring for each other. It is more joyful to see you all in peaceful harmony than to have any expensive perfume poured over my feet. Mary's love for me was great because I raised her brother Lazarus from the tomb. She was willing to pour the costly oil over my feet in gratitude for what I had done for her and her family. Life is more costly and more precious than any perfume that money can buy. Now go and do likewise to others as I have done for you.

My Jesus, I love you with my whole heart. Teach me to love you and others more and more each day.

BETRAYER

March 31

"Then Judas, his betrayer, said in reply, 'Surely it is not I, Rabbi?'" Matthew 26:25

It is the people who are closest to you who can hurt you the most. Learn from me. Forgive them and bless them until the end. Do not hold any grudges against them for they do not know what they are doing. Their vision is limited. Many of them are influenced by the culture and the environment around them. They do not see things with my eyes. But you do and you know my will. Be merciful and compassionate to those who betray you. Let your actions speak love to all. Do not act out of anger or hatred but from your loving heart. Love others as I have loved you, always forgiving and always caring.

Lord, give me more of your forgiving heart. I want to forgive others and to love them as you have loved me.

TRUSTING LAMB

April 1

"I am like a trusting lamb led to slaughter." Jeremiah 11:19

My precious child, suffering is part of growth. Without pain there is no gain or spiritual growth. Do not be afraid to pick up your cross and follow my example. I love even those who hated me. I forgave them for they did not know what they were doing. Most people do not try to hurt you intentionally unless they are really your enemies. Even then, I say to you, "Love your enemies." With love you will be able to soften all hearts. Come and follow me.

Lamb of God, you who take away the sins of the world, have mercy on me. Lord, give me the courage to carry my cross daily and follow you.

DENY ME

April 2

"The cock will not crow before you deny me three times."
John 13: 38

All human beings are imperfect. Only I am perfect. Your best friend will fail you. Only I will always be there for you. I am a forgiving God. I know all your struggles and weaknesses. I am not here to condemn you but to let you know that you are forgiven. I love you with an everlasting love. There will be nothing that can separate us. I will always be there for you. You can count on me. Even when you deny me as Peter did I will never stop loving you. I will never give up on you. You are mine. You can trust in me. Be transformed as Peter was. Do not turn to despair but have hope in me. I love you, my loving child.

Change me, Lord, and mold me into your image and likeness. I want to trust you more and more each day.

PASSOVER

April 3

"Before the Feast of Passover, Jesus knew that his hour had come to pass from this world to the Father." John 13:1

My dear child, every soul is precious to me. I served and I died for everyone willingly. It is only through my blood that you are saved. Just as with the Passover in Egypt only those households that had the blood of the lamb over their doorposts were saved. So it is with my blood. Those who eat my body and drink my blood will live forever in heaven with me. There will be no more sadness and weeping. Only joy will fill your heart. You will spend eternity with me. While you are here on earth, go and serve others as I have served you. Wash their feet, feed the hungry and dress the naked. But most important of all is to bring all souls closer to me.

Here I am, Lord. I come to serve you and others. Thank you for redeeming me with your precious blood.

OLD SELF

April 4

"We know that our old self was crucified with him, so that our sinful body might be done away with, that we might no longer be in slavery to sin." Romans 6:6

My child, your old self is gone, wiped clean by my precious blood and water. Your new self is everything I have created you to be – gentle, kind, loving, caring, compassionate, understanding, forgiving, comforting, patient, praising, self controlled, wise and thanksgiving. In every way you have become more and more like me. When people see you they will know that you are my child. They see the resemblance; like father like son; like mother like daughter. You are my precious child and that is your new self. Live each day in my love. There is no room for sadness, guilt or sin. There is only love, peace and joy.

My loving Father, thank you for sending your only Son into the world, so that I might be saved and enjoy eternity with you in heaven. It is such a privilege to be your child.

HE COMMISSIONED US

April 5

"He commissioned us to preach to the people and testify that he is the one appointed by God as judge of the living and the dead." Acts 10:42

I am as alive today as I was eons ago. I am the living God. Death has no power over me. Everyone who believes in me will be saved. So go and proclaim the good news to all. Do not be worried about what other people say or think. You are building my kingdom. Let no one stop you. When people laugh and ridicule you, you will be blessed because I know how faithful and obedient you really are. Do not let other people's comments hurt you. They do not know any better. They are not ready to receive me into their hearts. But you are commissioned to spread the seed for me. Whether the seed grows or not, it doesn't matter. Go forth and be my disciple.

Rejoice and be glad! For today my Lord has risen from the dead. He is my Savior and my redeemer. Thank you for calling me to be your disciple.

MARY MAGDALENE

April 6

"Mary Magdalene and the other Mary went away quickly from the tomb, fearful yet overjoyed, and ran to announce the news to his disciples." Matthew 28:8

Yes, my precious child, I chose to appear to women first because they were willing to step out of their comfort zone to go to the tomb to minister to me. They were not afraid to face the guards or to handle my dead body. Their love for me overcame all their fear. All they wanted was to see that I was properly buried. That is why I appeared to them first. I knew they would believe in me and would tell others the good news. They were faithful in all they did for me. They followed me throughout my ministry. They saw to all my needs. They were my right hand behind the scenes. They were just as important to me as were the twelve disciples. I can use you in the same way.

Lord, thank you for choosing me to spread your good news to others. Lead me and guide me. Protect me from all harm.

BE BAPTIZED

April 7

"Repent and be baptized, every one of you, in the name of Jesus Christ, for the forgiveness of your sins; and you will receive that gift of the Holy Spirit." Acts 2:38

My kingdom is very simple and easy to reach. Even a child can enter it. It doesn't require a PhD or hardship. All it takes is to love me with all your heart. Only love matters in my kingdom. Nothing else. Do not feel that you have to work hard to earn it. I have already earned it for you. True love is to be transparent to one another. True love is always ready to forgive. True love does everything with joy – even death on the cross. At baptism, the water washes away all your sins. Purifying your body and soul as a bride prepares herself for her husband. Only then will I be able to fill you up with my Holy Spirit.

Come, Holy Spirit, come! Come into my heart. Teach me to love God more and more each day.

STAY WITH US

April 8

"Stay with us, for it is nearly evening and the day is almost over." Luke 24:29

My loving child, how many times I have longed to be with you, but you were too busy with earthly things. I never enter into your heart without being first invited for I have given you a free will. I honor you and respect you. Therefore, before you start any project or go any place, invite me in first. Ask for my presence and I will guide you and teach you. You will be filled with my spirit of joy and confidence. You will be able to do all things for my glory. You will see the world as I see. Your life will be changed 180 degrees like that of the two disciples on the road to Emmaus. They were depressed and ready to head home before they met me on the road. But the minute they invited me to have supper with them they recognized me and knew exactly what they should do. They turned around and went back to Jerusalem to be witnesses to the eleven disciples.

Lord Jesus, I invite you into my heart. Never let me be separated from you. You are my all and my salvation. I love you.

GHOST

April 9

"Touch me and see, because a ghost does not have flesh and bones as you can see I have." Luke 24:39

Yes, I have risen. I am not a ghost. I am your Jesus with flesh and bone. When you die, you will have flesh and bone also. You will enjoy the banquet in heaven with me for eternity. There is nothing compared to the joy in heaven. All the tears will be wiped away for I am with you always. With me, your heart will be filled to the brim with my joy. A ghost is a wandering soul who is lost. You will not be lost, but found. You have a home in heaven with me. I have prepared a place especially for you. Your name is written in the book of life.

Lord, I can hardly wait for the day when I can see you face to face. Increase my faith in you, my loving Jesus.

THE RIGHT SIDE

April 10

"Cast the net over the right side of the boat and you will find something." John 21:6

My child, I am always standing close to you. But you are like my disciples who were too busy to notice me standing by the shore. They did not ask me to go with them on the boat when they went fishing. They caught nothing all night. When you are too busy with so many activities and forget to ask me for my guidance you will not accomplish much nor realize that I am standing close to you. Unless you stop to listen or search for me, you will not feel my presence. My child, from now on try to make a habit of asking me before you do anything. You will be amazed how fruitful your life will be with my presence. You will live an abundant life. Like my disciples, you will catch more than 153 large fish but they will not break your net. Come and enjoy the feast with me.

Jesus, you are truly present every minute of my life. Open my eyes so I may see you wherever I am. Help me to listen to your voice and to obey what you ask me to do.

BOLDNESS

April 11

"They were all filled with the Holy Spirit and began to proclaim God's message with boldness." Act 4:31

My precious child, to become bold is to step out without fear. When your love for me is greater than your love for others that is when you will become bold in sharing my story. The eleven disciples were willing to risk their lives for me because they loved me more than their family and friends. Your love for me must increase before you will have the courage to lay down your life for me. My disciples were my constant companions which means they spent every minute with me. Whether they were eating or sleeping, they were with me. They listened to my words and they did what I told them to do. I would like to invite you to be my companion too.

Lord Jesus, I want to love you above everyone else. Please come into my heart and live with me every moment of my life.

BORN FROM ABOVE

April 12

"Amen, Amen, I say to you, no one can see the kingdom of God without being born from above." John 3:3

People do not understand that in order to go into the Kingdom of God, one has to be born of water and spirit through baptism. It is like going to a foreign country. One must have a passport and visa. Without them one cannot go in. So it is with the Kingdom of God. It is very easy to be born of water and spirit. It is within everyone's reach. Everyone is invited to the kingdom of my Father. It is free to all. So go and tell everyone about this good news. Be loving. Be kind. It is a free gift for all who would like to spend eternity with me. Go and proclaim the good news to everyone who is not baptized. This is your vocation. This is your call.

Lord, give me the boldness to speak about you and your kingdom to everyone I meet. Fill me with your Holy Spirit. Fill me with your wisdom.

COMMUNITY OF BELIEVERS

April 13

"The community of believers was of one heart and mind, and no one claimed that any of his possessions was his own, but they had everything in common." Acts 4:32

When you were baptized, my child, you were born again into my family. Everyone who is baptized becomes your brother or sister. Everything you have comes from my Father. As a child, did you worry about anything? Did you lack anything? Did your parents provide for all your needs? This is the way your new life in my family should be, totally trusting and contented with everything you have. Since everything is given to you freely, you should share it with others in need. Only then are you truly living in my kingdom. You will lack for nothing. The more you give, the more you will receive. Be generous to all who are in need.

My God and my loving Father, I thank you for giving me a new life in your kingdom. I am truly blessed. Help me to share everything with those less fortunate than I am.

CHOSEN ONE

April 14

"Here is my servant whom I uphold, my chosen one with whom I am pleased, upon whom I have put my Spirit; he shall bring forth justice to the nations, not crying out, not shouting, not making his voice heard in the street." Isaiah 42:1

In my vision I saw a person carrying a heavy load on his back. Jesus said to me, "My child, you are chosen to help those who are heavily burdened and downtrodden. They cannot turn their lives around by themselves. You, my loving child, are called to lighten their burden and to do justice. You are my hands and feet. You are put on this earth to continue to do the work that I started 2,000 years ago. You are gifted to help others who cannot help themselves. They are like prisoners locked in their weakness and sin. Go and fill the gap with my love and compassion of everyone you meet today. Go with my Spirit."

Loving Jesus, I thank you for choosing me to do your work. Fill me with your Holy Spirit.

WRATH OF GOD

April 15

"Whoever believes in the Son has eternal life, but whoever disobeys the Son will not see life, but the wrath of God remains upon him." John 3:36

In my vision I saw God, the Father, raising his hand ready to strike down the sinners. But Jesus, the Divine Mercy, stood in front of his Father and from his hands water and blood poured out over the sinners. Jesus said to me, "Whoever comes to me will find mercy and redemption. I am a forgiving God. Everyone who repents his sins will be forgiven. The wrath is only for those who do not seek God, nor ask for his forgiveness. They are self-centered and think of themselves as gods. They do not obey my laws and commandments. My laws are created to give life. Whoever obeys them will have abundant life. Here are the key words to remember, my child: obedience, repentance, forgiveness and belief in my mercy and compassion."

Lord, have mercy. Christ, have mercy on me, a sinner. Jesus, wash me clean from all my past sins.

LIKE A CHILD

April 16

"Amen, I say to you, whoever does not accept the kingdom like a child will not enter it." Mark 10:15

It is easier to teach a child than an adult because a child is open and eager to learn. You are my child. I will teach you. I will show you the kingdom and you will bring others to me. Trust in me. Do not be anxious about anything. Learn from children. They never worry about what to eat or what to wear. Imagine yourself in their shoes. See how carefree they are. They enjoy each moment of their day. They love and forgive easily. They do not hold grudges. Let your heart sing with joy like a little child. It warms my heart to see you when you are happy.

My loving Father, I trust in you. Jesus, I love you. Holy Spirit, I am yours.

IT IS I

April 17

"It is I. Do not be afraid." John 6:20

Yes, I am God of the universe. I am a loving God. I came to show you the way to my Father who loves you with an everlasting love. You have nothing to fear. My Father created you in his image and likeness. He is very pleased with you. He loves all his creations, especially human beings. Every person is capable of great love. He has given you a free will to choose to love him or not. He even sent me into the world to model for you and to show you what true love is all about. So do not be afraid. Do not be concerned about your daily needs. My Father will provide them for you. All you have to do is to LOVE. Perfect love casts out all fear.

Open my heart, Lord. Come into my soul and teach me to love as you have loved me. With you at my side, I have nothing to fear.

OBEY GOD

April 18

"But Peter and the apostles said in reply, 'We must obey God rather than men.'" Acts 5:29

My dear child, to obey me is to love me. Love without obedience is self love. Only when you surrender your fears and anxieties to me can you truly do my will. Without obedience you are still self-centered. You still think that you can accomplish everything without me. Perfect love for God is to surrender and abandon your will to me. Only then will you be able to live in perfect harmony with yourself and with God. Your true self will only come into being when you are in total obedience to my will. My will for you is what gives you purpose for your life. You will find true happiness and peace when you obey my will.

Lord, here I am ready to do your will. Help me to be bold in proclaiming your kingdom to others. It is a joy to work for you.

GRACE AND POWER

April 19

"Now Stephen, filled with grace and power, was working great wonders and signs among the people." Acts 6:8

Stephen was filled with grace and power because he first emptied himself and surrendered his life to me. Without his first removing all his own ambition and power, I could not pour my love and the Holy Spirit upon him. You, my child, must make room for me by clearing everything from your heart. Like a pregnant woman preparing a room for her baby's arrival you first need to clean the baby's room by removing all the old furniture. Then you need to furnish it with everything new for the baby. You must do the same with your heart for me. You must first empty yourself and prepare yourself with spiritual food. Only then will you be ready to be filled with my grace, power, wisdom and inner joy. Your face will be like the face of an angel, full of love and peace.

Help me, Lord, to empty myself so your love and grace can be filled into my heart. Come Holy Spirit, come.

BREAD OF LIFE

April 20

"I am the bread of life; whoever comes to me will never hunger, and whoever believes in me will never thirst." John 6:35

My loving child, I am all you need. When you have me, you have everything. All you have to do is to come to me and believe in me. It is so simple and yet many people find it difficult to accept this. I am the life, the way and the truth. When you are with me your heart will be filled with love, peace and joy. You will be able to see others with my eyes and love others with my heart. You will never go hungry or thirsty. All you need to do is to ask and it will be given to you. Imagine yourself sitting on a sedan chair, carried by 4 people. Whatever you need, you just wave your hand or say a word. Your wish will be granted without delay. You are my beloved one. I hear your prayers and I will always answer them.

Lord, my heart is overflowing with joy, knowing how much you love me. Thank you for being my bread of life.

THE LIGHT

April 21

"Whoever lives the truth comes to the light, so that his works can be clearly seen as done in God." John 3: 21

In my vision I saw a big, round, bright light, pure and white. Jesus said to me, "I am the light of the world. Everyone who comes to the light is instantly connected to my light and becomes bright. The light will reveal the truth to you. When you are away from the light you will live in darkness. When you are connected to the light, you will have the power to do all that I did. I am like your battery charger. Without this battery, you have no life. You can do nothing. I am the vine and you are the branches. Abide in me and you shall live. I will prune you until you bear good fruit."

O Lord, you are my light. Come and shine on me. I want to live in the truth.

CHOSEN INSTRUMENT

April 22

"Go, for this man is a chosen instrument of mine to carry my name before Gentiles, kings, and Israelites. " Acts 9:15

In my vision I saw myself as a knife in God's hand. He used me to set the captives free. During surgery he used the knife to cut and remove all bad parts of the body. In daily life he used me to spread butter and jam on the bread. But when this knife is in the hand of the evil one it can wound and kill others. Jesus said to me, "My child, you are in my hands. It is your job as my chosen instrument to keep yourself clean and sharpened to be used at anytime. Your job is to be ready and to be obedient to my promptings. Always listen to my lead. I will guide you in every chore you do each day if you ask me first. Do not go forth and act alone. Go with me. Hold onto my hand."

Thank you, God, for this beautiful vision. Use me and be with me always.

THE PROUD

April 23

"God opposes the proud but bestows favor on the humble."
1 Peter 5:5b

My precious child, the reason I favor the humble is because they depend totally on me and will do things only under the guidance of the Holy Spirit. The proud people act on their own power and think that they do not need me. Be humble and know that I am God. I will be with you always. Without me you can do nothing. With me, all things are possible. Learn to lean on me always.

Loving Father, I am nothing without you. You are my all. Teach me to be humble in your sight.

MY FLESH

April 24

"I am the living bread that came down from heaven; whoever eats this bread will live forever; and the bread that I will give is my flesh for the life of the world." John 6: 51

In my vision I saw the host glowing with pure white light. It reflected the sun light. Everyone who consumed the host became aglow. Eventually I saw the circle of light glowing and glowing. Jesus said to me, "My precious child, when you receive my body and blood, you also receive the light of life. Have you noticed how holy people always have a glow around them? I am the light of the world. When you receive communion you also receive my light. The two go together. Stay close to me; otherwise your light will diminish when you are far away from me. Notice how Moses' face glowed so much that he had to wear a veil to cover it. Come and receive my flesh and blood daily and you will live an abundant life."

Lord, I am not worthy to receive you, but just say the word and I shall be healed. Please come and fill me with your light.

HEAR MY VOICE

April 25

"My sheep hear my voice; I know them and they follow me." John 10:27

My child, you do not have to worry ever. I will always take care of you for you are mine. You belong to me. No one can snatch you away from me. All you have to do is to listen to my voice and follow me. You will never be taken away from me. With me at your side you have nothing to fear. I will protect you from all harm. You are my beloved. I have treasured you and loved you from the day you were conceived in your mother's womb. Even if you walk in the dark valley, I will be there for you. You have a great future ahead of you. I have prepared a lavish banquet for you. We will spend eternity together. Come and spend quiet moments alone with me. You will always hear my voice when you are quiet.

Speak, Lord, I am listening. I love to hear your voice. Your voice is sweeter than honey.

RESENTFUL

April 26

"Why are you so resentful and crestfallen? If you do well, you can hold up your head; but if not, sin is a demon lurking at the door: his urge is toward you, yet you can be his master." Genesis 4:6-7

My precious child, when you have negative feelings against your neighbor try to turn your thoughts to positive again. Feelings of resentment and hatred quickly open doors to the evil one. Resentment towards someone is the opposite of loving someone. When you feel resentful your heart will be hardened. See how Cain finally killed his brother Abel because of his jealousy and resentment. Instead of giving God the best of his fruits as his offering he gave only the minimum. His love for God was very shallow. Instead of improving his own behavior he killed his brother. My Father knows what is in your heart before you speak. Choose love always.

Lord, please forgive me for all the times that I have felt resentful towards others. Help me to love more like you.

THE GATE

April 27

"I am the gate. Whoever enters through me will be saved, and will come in and go out and find pasture." John 10:9

In my vision I saw a white gate and fence which enclosed an area of lush green pasture. Birds were singing. Outside the gate there was a forest, full of trees and darkness. Jesus said to me, "My child, I enclose you with my love inside the gate. You are protected from all harm and from the evil one. You are safe as long as you stay with me. Do not be tempted to wander off outside the gate where the evil one is ready to devour anyone who will follow him. Stay close to me. This way you will always be in good company. You will never have to worry about anything when you are with me."

Thank you, Jesus, for being my good shepherd. I will never try to wander off outside of your gate alone. I love you with my whole heart.

MY FATHER

April 28

"My Father, who has given them to me, is greater than all, and no one can take them out of the Father's hand. The Father and I are one." John 10:29-30

In my vision I saw a set of twins who were attached to each other in parts of their bodies. Jesus said to me, "Yes, my Father and I have existed together since the beginning of time. Like the twins, we are connected in spirit. Whatever my Father wants me to do, I will do. We are one. Even though we are two separate persons our thoughts are the same. Our love for you is the same. Our will is the same. When you love me, you are loving my Father. When you love my Father, you are also loving me. We are one God who has created this universe. You are our child and we love you."

My loving Father, I only want to do your will. Be with me, Jesus, and fill me with the Holy Spirit.

DO NOT CONDEMN

April 29

"And if anyone hears my words and does not observe them, I do not condemn him, for I did not come to condemn the world but to save the world." John 12:47

My precious child, do not point a finger at anyone. Every time one finger accuses others, three other fingers are pointing back at yourself. In this world everyone makes mistakes. No one is perfect. Your job is to see the good in everyone you encounter each day. Let them know how special and loved by God they are, for each soul is precious to me. Each soul is like a raw stone that could be a diamond after I polish it. Everyone is at a different stage of polishing. Some are already brilliant and shining; some are just at the beginning of their journey and process. Be patient with everyone. Be loving and forgiving to all. Be an imitator of me. Love each one as I have loved you.

Lord, give me your patience, loving kindness and your forgiveness for all who are in my life each day. Pour more of your love into my heart.

THE WAY

April 30

"I am the way and the truth and the life. No one comes to the Father except through me." John 14:6

In my vision I saw a yellow brick road like the Wizard of Oz movie. Jesus said to me, "My precious child, I am the way to my Father. If you follow me you will come to the Father. I am the truth, for this reason whatever I say to you, you can depend on it. I will never lead you astray. I am the life. Anyone who follows me will have abundant life, a life filled with joy and fulfillment, a life with purpose and meaning. You will never regret following me. My Father will reward you greatly. He will welcome you into his arms as I have already done. You will know him as well as I know him and you will be loved by him as he loves me."

Eternal Father, thank you for sending your only Son into the world so that I will know you and love you. Jesus, I am ready to let go of everything here on earth and to follow you into eternal life in heaven. Lead me to your Father.

IN MY NAME

May 1

"If you ask anything of me in my name, I will do it." John 14:14

My precious child, would you refuse anything your children ask of you? No, unless you know it is bad for them. So it is with me. Anything you ask of me, I will do it, unless I know it is not good for you. The closer the relationship with your family member or friends, the easier it is for you to ask of them a favor because you know how much they love and care about you. So it is with you and me. The most important thing is relationship. Can a loving mother refuse her baby her milk? No, because the baby belongs to her. The baby is of her own flesh and blood. So it is with you and me. You are my own flesh and blood for you eat my body and drink my blood every morning at Mass. You belong to me. I will never refuse you anything when you ask me in my name.

Lord, thank you for loving me so much and treating me as a part of your own body. I feel so blessed to be a member of your family.

NEW COMMANDMENT

May 2

"I give you a new commandment: love one another. As I have loved you, so you also should love one another." John 13:34

In my vision I saw a red heart and a white host. Jesus said to me, "My loving child, every time you receive me at the Eucharist my white host will replace the selfish cells in your heart. The more you receive me the more I will be able to work with your heart. Eventually your heart will be transformed into a pure white selfless heart like mine. You will be able to love others as I have loved you. You will be able to do sacrifices and not complain, but to do them with love and joy. I will renew your love and refresh your heart. You will be filled with my love."

Thank you, Jesus, for your love and this beautiful vision. I will always treasure it in my heart. I love you, Lord.

THE FATHER

May 3

"Believe me when I say that I am in the Father and the Father is in me." John 14:11

The Father and I are one. Since you receive me every morning at communion you also receive the Father. We are always united for I came into the world to do my Father's will. When we dwell in you, you too will be united with us and will do our will. It is through this unity that you will become our faithful disciple. Everything you do will be effective. No act will be useless. United, we can conquer the world. Invite us to dwell in you every morning. Do not leave your bed until you have invited us to join you each day. We are with you every minute and will guide you in all you do for us. You are our beloved child. Go in peace.

Lord, I invite you today and every day to come into my heart. May I be obedient to all your prompting. Father, I am here to do your will. Give me the courage to step out of my comfort zone.

HARDSHIP

May 4

"It is necessary for us to undergo many hardships to enter the kingdom of God." Acts 14:22

My beloved child, there is no true love without sacrifice. There is no building unless people spend time and effort building it. So it is with discipleship. Paul was willing to be stoned, put into prison in chains and go through a shipwreck. You will be purified and strengthened by going through hardship in order to prepare you for the kingdom of God. It is worth all your effort and sacrifice. While you are here on earth, do not let a day go by without doing good for others in my name. Do not miss any opportunity to tell everyone about the kingdom that I have prepared for each one of them.

Here I am, Lord, I come to do your will. Be with me each day. Show me the way. Give me the strength to overcome all hardship.

VINE GROWER

May 5

"I am the true vine, and my Father is the vine grower." John 15:1

In my vision I saw a vineyard. There was a large tree in the middle – the tree of life – it is Jesus. Jesus said to me, "My precious child, I am the vine and you are the branches. As long as you remain with me you will bear much fruit, for my tree will give you abundant life. You will experience true peace, love and joy in your heart. Away from me, you will be barren and useless, fit only to be thrown away and be burned. Abide in me; dwell in me and imitate me. My Father, who is the vine grower will prune you and nourish you with living water. You will bloom and grow."

Lord Jesus, I can do nothing without you. I need you in my life. I belong to you.

EVERYONE WHO BELIEVES

May 6

"I came into the world as light, so that everyone who believes in me might not remain in darkness." John 12:46

In my vision I saw Jesus walking in front of me, guiding me with his light. Jesus said to me, "The closer you come to me, the clearer you will be able to see the truth, for I am the light of the world. With me, you will see everything as in broad daylight. Nothing will be hidden from you because you believe in me. Those who do not believe do not see the truth and they walk in darkness and chaos. But you have the light in front of you to guide you on the right path. You will not stumble and fall. You will have the light of life."

I do believe in you, Lord. You are the light of the world. I will follow you always.

PAUL AND BARNABAS

May 7

"They listened while Paul and Barnabas described the signs and wonders God had worked among the Gentiles through them." Acts 15:12

I did many signs and wonders through my two disciples Paul and Barnabas because they were my faithful servants. Actually, you can see signs and wonders everywhere in this world. Look around at nature; there even greater signs and wonders surround you. For me, nothing is impossible. Even in Death Valley beautiful flowers will bloom. I have conquered death. There is always rebirth and renewal. I give life to all those who are hopeless. I give joy to those who are depressed. I give encouragement to those who have given up hope. I will work many more signs and wonders if you go and do my work for others. You will never come back empty-handed. You will return to me with joy and laughter for I am an awesome and almighty God.

I praise you, my God of the Universe. I praise you, the creator of all the angels and saints. All things are possible with you, Lord.

MY FRIENDS

May 8

"You are my friends if you do what I command you." John 15:14

Beloved, you are my friend. I have chosen you and you have answered my call. You can depend on me anytime just as you do with your friends. You can pour your heart out and I will listen and console you. You can trust in me in times of need. I will always be there for you. You can celebrate and rejoice with me. You can cry on my shoulder and I will comfort you. You can ask favors from me and I will not refuse you. I am your best friend. You can always count on me. Even though your friends might fail you, I will always be there for you. That is what true friendship is all about. So come to me in all your needs. I am with you, my child.

Thank you, Jesus. You are the best friend anyone can have. I love you with all my heart and soul.

WORLD HATES YOU

May 9

"If the world hates you, realize that it hated me first." John 15:18

In my vision I saw Jesus with all his light and glory. His enemies were all afraid of him. They hated the light as the cockroaches do. When they saw the light they all scattered. Jesus said to me, "My loving child, I am the light of the world. But the world prefers darkness, because in the dark of night they can do all evil things. The light reveals all their sinful deeds. It is the same with you. When your light shines towards people, those who are in darkness do not want to be near you. They are jealous of you and they hate you for exposing their sinfulness. But do not be afraid. I stand beside you. Let your light be a beacon for those who are lost and need guidance."

Jesus, let your light shine upon the entire world. Help me to stand firm in your light.

I IN HIM

May 10

"I am the vine, you are the branches. Whoever remains in me and I in him will bear much fruit, because without me you can do nothing." John 15:5

In my vision when I was living in Jesus, his body encased me completely like an astronaut suit. The minute I went too far away from him my air supply stopped flowing. As long as I was close to Jesus I breathed and lived in him. Jesus said to me, "My precious child, I live in your heart and you are living in my heart. When you wander off alone, then I cannot support you. When you live in me, all your actions are no longer your own. That is when they become mine. Everything we do together as one will bear much fruit."

Lord Jesus, never let me be separated from you. You are my life and my salvation. You are all I need.

TEACH YOU EVERYTHING

May 11

"The Advocate, the Holy Spirit that the Father will send in my name - he will teach you everything and remind you of all that I told you." John 14:26

My precious child, the Holy Spirit is the wisdom of God. When you have the Holy Spirit you will be able to see everything clearly through God's eyes. You will know the truth. You will be able to discern what is right from wrong. He will guide you in the right direction and say the right words at the right time. You will be able to love and heal as I did. So call on the Holy Spirit often. Invoke my name and I will send the Holy Spirit upon you. He will teach you everything.

Come Holy Spirit, come. Fill me with your wisdom. Teach me God's way and show me the path.

WILL NEVER THIRST

May 12

"Whoever drinks the water I shall give will never thirst; the water I shall give will become in him a spring of water welling up to eternal life." John 4: 14

The water I give you is free and is always there for you, my precious child. But you have to come and ask for it. My water will refresh and renew your soul. It will cleanse all your sins. It will give you the strength and the energy to do my work. It will satisfy not only your spiritual needs but also all your physical needs. Without my water, which is the Word of God, you will have no life in you. You shall perish. Come and drink my water daily, my child.

Lord, you are the living water. Give me your water so that my soul will never thirst again for you.

LAMP

May 13

"The city had no need of sun or moon to shine on it, for the glory of God gave it light, and its lamp was the Lamb." Revelation 21:23

In my vision I saw a lamp in the shape of a very bright shining cross. Anyone who touches the cross becomes as shining and bright as the cross. Jesus said to me, "My precious child, anyone who comes forward and touches me will have the same light as I have. Bring each soul to me so they may be enlightened. I want to see the whole world aglow with my light. Everyone who knows me and who has touched me will be able to give my light to all those in darkness. My light will remove all the dark areas of the soul. My light will show you the right path. My light will bring love and joy to your heart. Come and touch my light. Be one with me. Let your light shine."

Thank you, Jesus, for such a beautiful vision. Let me never be too tired to bring others to your light. Fill me with your light.

THE ADVOCATE

May 14

"If I do not go, the Advocate will not come to you. But if I go, I will send him to you." John 16:7

My loving child, you have the Advocate in you when you are baptized as a child. You believe in me and you have asked for the Advocate. Anyone who asks for the Holy Spirit will be given all that is requested. It is my desire that everyone be filled with my Spirit. The Holy Spirit and I are one, just as my Father and I are one. We will come and dwell in you. All you need to do is to invite us into your heart. The Advocate will comfort you and guide you. He will show you the Way. He will protect you from all harm, for I have already conquered the evil one. I came into the world so as to overcome death and sin. You are set free, my child. Receive my Holy Spirit, the Advocate.

My loving Jesus, fill me with your Advocate. I need your wisdom and knowledge. I need your guidance and protection. Come Holy Spirit, come.

SPIRIT OF TRUTH

May 15

"When he comes, the Spirit of truth, he will guide you to all truth." John 16:13

The opposite of truth is the lie. I am the truth and my enemy, the evil one, is the lie. If you follow me, the truth will set you free. If you follow the lie, it will destroy you. You will have no life in you. Living in the truth is like living in the light. You will have peace, love and joy. Living in the lie and deceit, you will experience agony, fear, suffering, depression and ultimately death. My loving child, be filled with my Spirit of truth. He will guide you and lead you to eternal life. He will give you knowledge and wisdom in all you do. He will give you the courage and the freedom to follow me daily.

Thank you, Jesus, for showing me the Spirit of truth. You are my Lord and my God. I love you and I adore you.

HEAVEN

May 16

"As he blessed them he parted from them and was taken up to heaven." Luke 24:51

Even though I was leaving my disciples, they were filled with joy for they had witnessed not only my humanity, but also my divine nature. They knew I was going to my Father. They rejoiced because they knew I was going to prepare a place for them in heaven. You are also to rejoice because I am preparing a place for you in my heart. My heart is your heaven. My heart is where joy, peace and love reside. Be not afraid. You are always in my heart. You are protected from all harm. Heaven is where I am. Whenever you are in my presence, you are in heaven. Come to me, my child.

Lord Jesus, with you there is perfect love, peace and joy. I want to be with you always.

LOVE ONE ANOTHER

May 17

"This is my commandment: love one another as I love you."
John 15:12

My loving child, I did not ask you to love the entire universe. I said to love one another as I love you. It is easier to love one person at a time. When you are with that person, give him or her all your love and attention. Be selfless. Be patient. Be understanding and compassionate. Give that person your full attention. Do not criticize or give advice, unless asked. People are hungry to be heard. People need someone who really cares about them and loves them just the way they are. Only your full acceptance of their weaknesses and imperfections will inspire them to change. Go and be my love for them. I love you with all my heart.

I love you too, my God and my Savior. Never let me be separated from your love.

WHATEVER YOU ASK

May 18

"Amen, amen, I say to you, whatever you ask the Father in my name he will give you." John 16:23

The Father and I are one. We have a very close and loving relationship. That is why whatever you ask in my name, the Father will give to you. He will not refuse you anything. That is the kind of love relationship that I desire from you. I want to be so close to you that you can ask me for anything and I will give it to you. Remember when you asked your brother to donate money for remodeling a chapel? You knew in your heart that he would give you whatever you asked of him, because he loves you and he knows how much you love him. That is the kind of love and trust that I want you to experience with me. You can come to me and ask of me anything and I will never refuse you. You can count on me and on my Father.

Lord, you are such a loving and awesome God. I want to trust in you and not be afraid to come to you for anything.

TO BE SAVED

May 19

"What must I do to be saved?" Acts 16:30

Everyone who believes in me will be saved. It seems to be so simple. But it is true. I have come into the world to save, not to condemn. It is my desire that everyone will be able to join me at the heavenly banquet. However, many are too busy with this world and choose to do their own will. But you, my beloved, have chosen to believe in me and to do my will. I have prepared a special place for you in heaven.

Lord Jesus, I do believe in you with my whole heart and my whole soul. Increase my faith in you. You are the Savior of the world.

SPEAKING IN TONGUES

May 20

"For they could hear them speaking in tongues and glorifying God." Acts 10:46

My precious child, when you are filled with the Holy Spirit you will be able to do the things that I want you to do even though you may not understand them. The gift of tongues is a perfect example of totally surrendering yourself to my will. The more you surrender yourself to me, the more I will be able to use you. Speaking in tongues is one of the gifts I give to those who are willing to trust me and to do my will. When you are speaking in tongues, you are glorifying God.

Lord, send forth your Spirit so that I will be filled with your love for others. I want to praise you and glorify you in all I do.

POWER

May 21

"You will receive power when the Holy Spirit comes upon you, and you will be witnesses in Jerusalem, throughout Judea and Samaria, and to the ends of the earth." Acts 1:8

My child, you must be open to receive power from my Father. Ask and invite the Holy Spirit to be with you each day. You need to be filled with his power and love every morning before you are ready to go out and do his work. Without the power of the Holy Spirit you can do nothing that is pleasing to God. Only through his guidance and wisdom will you then be his true disciple. He will empower you with his gifts so that you will be able to do great works for him. These works will last. They are works that will bring honor and glory to God the Father. Go in peace and joy.

Come, Holy Spirit and fill my heart with your loving power. I can do nothing without you. With you all things are possible.

I GLORIFIED YOU

May 22

"I glorified you on earth by accomplishing the work that you gave me to do." John 17:4

Sing a new song to us every day, my child. Your praises give glory to us. Let your heart be united with ours. Let your eyes see the world as we see it. Let your hands do the work that we have planned for you to do. Let your feet walk on holy ground. Where we are, there you shall be. To give glory to us is to do the work that we want to be accomplished. Do not have any anxiety whatsoever because we are with you. You will accomplish everything we have planned for you. So do not worry. All will be done according to our will. Just keep close to us and we will guide you and support you in all your needs.

Lord, may all the angels and the saints glorify you. May all the heavenly hosts sing alleluia to you. I praise you and glorify you, Father, Son and Holy Spirit.

MORE BLESSED

May 23

"Keep in mind the words of the Lord Jesus who himself said, 'It is more blessed to give than to receive.'" Acts 20:35

In my vision I saw a river that was flowing and full of living creatures and fish. While in a dead lake – like the Dead Sea – there was nothing alive living in it. Jesus said to me, "My precious child, the more you give away the more I can do the miracle of multiplication. You will be like the little boy who shared his five loaves and two fish. Right in front of his eyes he saw one of my miracles. He could not believe that his small amount of food could feed 5,000 people and still have plenty left over. Do you see his face beaming with joy and astonishment? This is what I want you to do too. Share what little you have with all those who are in need. I will reward you abundantly."

Give me a generous heart, Lord. Change me and mold me into your image and likeness. I want to give and to share what I have with others like that little boy.

YOU KNOW EVERYTHING

May 24

"Lord, you know everything; you know that I love you." Jesus said to him, "Feed my sheep." John 21:17

My loving child, there is nothing you do, say or think that is hidden from me. I know you better than anyone you love. I knew you from your mother's womb. I have heard you cry when you were deeply hurt by others. I felt your suffering and pain when you were very sick and weak. I was there when you felt so alone and no one cared about you. I understand you better than anyone else on earth. How can I not love you? I have nursed you to health. I have saved you out of darkness. I have taught you everything you know. You are mine. Now go and feed my sheep as Peter did. Come and follow me.

Lord Jesus, you are the love of my life. You are my best friend. You are the center of my life. I will follow you always.

STRONG DRIVING WIND

May 25

"Suddenly there came from the sky a noise like a strong driving wind, and it filled the entire house in which they were." Acts 2:2

My child, I did not come to destroy but to build. The hurricanes destroy everything they touch. My strong driving wind, which is the Holy Spirit, will build my church. It was on that Pentecost day that my disciples were given the courage and the strength to go out and to proclaim the good news to all. That was the morning when my disciples converted 3,000 people. I want to do the same now with you and your family. Be patient, be open and be willing to be filled by my Spirit. It will come like a strong driving wind.

I invite you Jesus and the Holy Spirit to come into my entire family. You are our hope and our salvation.

BE HOLY

May 26

"Be holy yourselves in every aspect of your conduct, for it is written, 'Be holy because I am holy.'" 1 Peter 1: 16

My love, to be holy is to do every action with me in mind. Every action should be loving and caring. Let compassion and mercy be your foremost conduct. Let my agenda for you each day become your agenda. Let every work you do glorify my Father in heaven. Let your love and forgiveness shine through. When people see you, they will see me. When people ask for help or healing, you will drop whatever you are doing and go forth to be there for them. This is what I did while I was on earth. Every action I did I checked with my Father first and then I followed through. My goal was to conquer evil with love. I want everyone to be saved. Go and do likewise.

Lord, fill me with more of your love and wisdom. Help me to be like you in everything I do and say each day.

THE CUP

May 27

"The cup that I drink, you will drink and with the baptism with which I am baptized, you will be baptized." Mark 10:39

The cup that I will give you, my loving child, is my precious blood. You will never have to suffer more than you can endure. My body and blood will sustain you. I will carry you in my arms when you can no longer walk. I will give you the strength and the courage to drink the cup that I have planned for you. So do not have any worry or anxiety. I will be with you always for you are as precious to me as your children are to you. I will always protect you from all harm. I will shelter you under my wings. Trust in me.

Here I am, Lord. I thank you for your precious body and blood to sustain me each day.

GOOD CONDUCT

May 28

"Maintain good conduct among the Gentiles, so that if they speak of you as evildoers, they may observe your good works and glorify God on the day of visitation." 1 Peter 2:12

Always return evil with good, my child. Do not hold any grudges against anyone. Be merciful and understanding. Be loving. Return hatred with loving acts. Your actions speak louder than words. The truth will set you free. You don't have to defend yourself when you are falsely accused. Continue to do good. Continue to be helpful to all those in need. When people ask you for something, be generous. When they ask you to pray, lay hands on them. When they are sick, visit them and pray for healing. When they are hungry, feed them. When they are depressed, cheer them up and give them hope. But most of all, love them the way I love you. Be my hands and feet to them.

Yes, Lord, I will do good to all who ask for my help, even those who do not love me. Fill me with your love for them.

BELIEVE

May 29

"I tell you, all that you ask for in prayer, believe that you will receive it and it shall be yours." Mark 11:24

My precious child, do you believe that everything is possible with me? I have created this entire universe. Do you think that I will not be able to provide for you whatever you ask of me? Do you believe that I love you? Do you believe that I will refuse anything you ask of me? Have you refused anything that your children or loved ones ask of you? Do you always grant their wishes? Do you understand now why when you ask for anything in prayer, it shall be yours? Do you still doubt that I love you? Do you think I can refuse you anything? Remember that I died on the cross for you. I laid down my life for you. Believe in me with your whole heart, my little one.

Yes, Lord, I do believe in you. Help me to trust in you more and more each day.

ALL TRUTH

May 30

"When he comes, the Spirit of truth, he will guide you to all truth." John 16:12

My Holy Spirit will teach you all things for he is the wisdom of truth. I sent him to you so as to enlighten your mind and to lead you on the right path. He will reveal to you the truth about us and about the universe. You will see things in a different light. You will understand the truth and follow it. The truth will set you free. You will feel such joy when you know the truth about us. My Father, Holy Spirit and I are one God but three persons. Our love for each other is more than you can ever comprehend. When you love others as we love you, you have a touch of truth. You will experience such joy and peace when you have the Spirit of truth. So, ask for the Holy Spirit to come into your life daily. Let him guide you in all you do.

Spirit of the living God, fall afresh on me. Mold me and guide me to your holy will.

GENEROSITY

May 31

"Great is the generosity you showed me today, when the Lord delivered me into your grasp and you did not kill me."
1 Samuel 24:18

My child, love your enemies. Pour blessings upon them. Only in this way will you be able to change their hearts. Love heals. Love melts the hateful heart. Be generous to all, especially those who are in need of love. Those people lack love because they have not been loved. They are searching for love all in the wrong places. Only I can give them what is lacking. So go and be my loving heart to them. Pour your love and compassion upon them. Anoint them with my blessings. Pray for them constantly. Forgive them for what they have done to you. Do not hold any grudges or resentment against them. Just love them with my kind and merciful heart.

My Jesus, please give me a generous heart like yours so that I will be able to love everyone like you. Enlarge my heart, Lord.

CONFIDENCE IN GOD

June 1

"We have confidence in God, that if we ask anything according to his will, he hears us." 1 John 5:14

In my vision I was standing in line getting ready for a battle. The enemies were all lined up facing me. When I looked up, I saw a huge giant standing by my side. Seeing the giant, the enemies all ran away scared. Jesus said to me, "My child, have confidence in me. When you have me on your side you have nothing to fear. No evil will touch you. You can go forth with me protecting you and guiding you on the right path. You will win one battle after another. I hear all your prayers and will answer them even before you speak. Fear not, I am with you every step of the way. I know your future and all your needs. You have nothing to worry about. Live each day to the fullest. Live with me by your side."

Lord, with you I have no fear. I know you are always there protecting me from the evil one. I surrender my life into your hands.

SURPLUS WEALTH

June 2

"For they have all contributed from their surplus wealth, but she, from her poverty, has contributed all she had, her whole livelihood." Mark 12:44

This is a lesson in not judging another's actions, my loving child. This poor widow gave only two small coins and yet she gave more than the rich people who gave large sums. Sometimes people judge others too quickly not knowing their intention and motive. Each person can only give what he has. Sometimes what he has is only very little. But I know each person's heart and where he comes from. Therefore, only I can be a fair judge to all. Learn from this story and be generous in your giving, not just from your surplus wealth, but from your heart. When you give from your heart, you give with love. And only by giving in this way will you be rewarded by my Father.

Lord Jesus, give me a generous and loving heart. Help me to be more and more like you each day. Help me to never judge another person.

HAUGHTY

June 3

"Have the same regard for one another; do not be haughty but associate with the lowly; do not be wise in your own estimation." Romans 12:16

My child, everyone is precious to me. That is why you need to treat each one with love and respect. Do not feel that you are better than others for I have given each one different talent and gifts. Each one is unique. So do not feel yourself better and smarter than others. Mary, my mother, was carrying me in her womb and yet she went in haste to help her cousin Elizabeth. She did not act as though she were better than Elizabeth, who was carrying John in her womb. My mother rejoiced with her and comforted her. She even washed and cooked for Elizabeth while she was there for 3 months. She did all the menial chores as a servant and helped her cousin during those difficult months. Imitate my mother. Give every work you do for the honor and glory of God.

Mary, my mother, pray for me that I will be like you in serving others. Lord, give me a humble and loving heart.

NEW EARTH

June 4

"But according to his promise we await new heavens and a new earth in which righteousness dwells." 2 Peter 3:13

In the new heavens and in the new earth there will be no more tears and suffering. Only those whose heart is like mine will be in heaven. Everyone will be loving, caring and compassionate. Everyone will be looking after the other's needs. It will be total bliss and joy for love is joy. My loving child, have you seen a newly married couple going on their honeymoon? What joy! What bliss! So it is when you enter into the new heavens and the new earth. You will find perfect harmony and perfect love. You will be pampered and loved by everyone there, especially by me, my Father and the Holy Spirit.

Take me there, Lord. I am ready to be with you for eternity. I can hardly wait for the day to see the new heavens and the new earth.

ALL YOUR HEART

June 5

"You shall love the Lord your God with all your heart, with all your soul, with all your mind, and all your strength." Mark 12:30

My precious child, your love for me will grow. Like a baby, first he finds his own hand. He admires it and examines it. Eventually he notices your hand and he puts it into his mouth. He tastes it and licks it. The baby does not do anything for others until he grows up and matures. As a child of two years old, he only thinks about himself – me, myself and I. Many people are stuck at this stage. Until people learn to sacrifice for others they will not mature into loving and caring persons. Keep progressing each day towards perfection in love. Think more and more about others rather than yourself. Put others ahead of your own needs. Only then can you love others as much as I have loved you.

Lord Jesus, I need more of your love and kindness. Change my selfish heart into a generous and loving heart like yours.

ALL SCRIPTURE

June 6

"All Scripture is inspired by God and is useful for teaching, for refutation, for correction, and for training in righteousness, so that one who belongs to God may be competent, equipped for every good work." 2 Timothy 3:16-17

In my vision I saw a treasure chest filled with pearls, gold coins and beautiful jewelry. Jesus said to me, "My precious child, the scripture is like a treasure chest. Everything in it is precious and priceless. My words have power and will not return empty. I have created the entire universe through my spoken words. My words can heal and destroy. When I cursed the fig tree its roots were destroyed. No one ever ate a fig from that tree again. When I bless, my blessings go down to thousands of generations. So study the scripture every day. Treasure every word you read for they are truly my words to you. They guide you in everything you do. You and your entire family will be blessed when you read my scripture."

Lord, thy word is a lamp unto my feet and a light unto my path. Thank you, Lord, for giving me your scripture. I treasure it more than gold.

SEVENFOLD

June 7

"For the Lord always repays and he will give back to you sevenfold." Sirach 35:11

In my vision I saw a person singing inside a cave. The echo of his voice came back to him many times. Jesus said to me, "My child, for every little thing you do for others, my heavenly Father will reward you seven times more. For every gift you give to others, more will be given back to you. It is like a small stone thrown into the water which causes the ripple effect. So it is that every kindness, patience and generosity you have shown to others will have the same result. My Father sees every good deed you do for others. Do not let one day go by without being kind and generous to everyone in need. He will repay you in heaven."

Lord, increase my effort to help others in need. Enlarge my heart and help me to be more and more like you.

CLEAN OF HEART

June 8

"Blessed are the clean of heart, for they will see God." Matthew 5:8

My loving child, a person with a clean heart is one who loves without ceasing, one who has no evil thoughts in her heart. She is one who loves until it hurts with a heart full of compassion and mercy. A transparent heart is one without any blemishes, a heart that stands firm in the truth and in God. A clean heart is one which is able to love and to forgive. Imitate my heart and my mother's heart. See how our hearts are both filled with red blood – full of love and compassion for all. Our hearts were wounded, but that did not stop us from loving and giving. As my blood flows out from my side, so does my love for you. Only a clean heart will see the face of God.

O Jesus, have mercy on me. Please give me more of your love so that I will be able to love others as you love me.

WITH YOU

June 9

"I am with you always, until the end of the age." Matthew 28:20

I am not only with you but also in you, my child. I live in your heart. You are mine. I will always be there for you. Call on me often and ask for my assistance in all you do. I am closer to you than any person on earth. I know every thought that is in your mind. I know all your desires and frustrations. I know when you are happy and sad. I am always by your side, comforting you, guiding you and loving you. Can you feel my presence in you?

Thank you, Lord, for always being there for me. Jesus, I know you will never leave me or forsake me. I love you, Jesus, and I trust in you.

GREATEST

June 10

"Whoever obeys and teaches these commandments will be called greatest in the kingdom of heaven." Matthew 5:19

In my vision I saw a toy that I used to make when I was growing up. It was a toy made from a spool of thread. We carved a zigzag pattern on each end of the spool and added a small nail on one end. We wound a rubber band through the hole onto a stick. Without the carving the spool would have been too smooth and could not climb any books or any other objects. With the carving, it could climb and go places. Jesus said to me, "So it is with my commandments. Without obeying my commandments, it is impossible to enter into my kingdom. To love me is to follow my commandments. Without the commandments carved in your heart, it is impossible to be holy and blameless. You will be able to enter into my kingdom with love. Love and commandments go hand in hand. Love without the commandments is like an empty gong. Love for others is what my kingdom is all about. There are only two commandments: love God with your whole heart, mind, soul and strength. The second commandment is to love your neighbor as yourself. Go and teach others about my love and my commandments."

Loving Jesus, to obey your commandments is my delight. Help me to share your love with others.

ANGRY

June 11

"Whoever is angry with his brother will be liable to judgment." Matthew 5:22

My precious child, imitate me. I was never angry with people, even when they were persecuting me. I love everyone. I did condemn their behavior, but I never was angry with them personally. I was angry when I saw what the merchants had done to my Father's house. I drove the money changers away from the temple for I did not want them to turn my Father's house into a market place. Always hate the sin and not the sinner. Anger will only ruin your own health. Unforgiving anger will turn into resentment. Anger festered in your body will be as harmful as cancer. You must deal with your anger right away. Do not let the sun go down on your anger. Ask me to remove all that is hurting you. Otherwise it will ruin your health and your life. Let me heal your anger.

Lord, I have forgiven everyone who has hurt me in the past. I refuse to hold onto any anger against anyone. I want to love like you.

HER HEART

June 12

"His mother kept all these things in her heart." Luke 2:51

My mother and I only do what my Father tells us to do. We are united together in mind and in heart. We live each day for my Father's honor and glory. We pray, we listen and we do his Will. My mother and I have only one purpose in mind, which is to do what the Holy Spirit tells us to do. We love each one of you with our whole heart. We want each one of you to be united with us in heaven for eternity. We are always at your side when you need us. We will help you to turn every day's chores into joyful miracles. Call on us often. We will answer you and help you. You can count on us.

Loving Jesus, I give my heart to you. Enlarge my heart, O Lord.

SALT

June 13

"You are the salt of the earth. But if salt loses its taste, with what can it be seasoned? It is no longer good for anything but to be thrown out and trampled underfoot." Matthew 5:13

Salt is a precious commodity. It was worth as much as gold in ancient times because it preserves food, it enhances taste and it kills germs. Like the gift of the Holy Spirit, it heals, it restores and it brings love, peace and joy to others. My precious child, you were given many gifts from the Holy Spirit at your baptism. Go and be the salt of the earth for others. Your mission is to preserve every soul, enhance their spiritual life and deliver them from the evil one.

Lord, here I am, ready to do your Will. Fill me with your Holy Spirit.

MY LOST SHEEP

June 14

"Rejoice with me because I have found my lost sheep." Luke 15:6

See how joyful we are in heaven when one sinner repents and is brought back to the right path. My child, go and find the lost sheep for me. They are lost. They have wandered away from me not knowingly. Please go and bring them back. Help them to find the right path. Put them on your shoulder and carry them back to me. There will be great rejoicing and celebration for each soul you bring back to the fold. You are my hands and feet now. You are my heart to love all those who are hurting and blind to my love. You are my mouth to tell my story of love to all you meet. Will you go and find my lost sheep? Will you go and bring them back to me?

Yes, Lord, I will go and find the lost sheep and bring them back to you. I want to bring the good news to them for you.

SINS ARE FORGIVEN

June 15

"Then Jesus said to the woman, 'Your sins are forgiven.'" Luke 7:48

My loving child, I know how you feel every time when you realize you have sinned. It is through repentance that you grow closer to me. Through forgiveness you will know how much I love you. I have paid for all your sins with my suffering and I have nailed them to my cross. Nothing can separate us now. All you need to do is to come to me and ask for forgiveness like that woman who washed my feet with her tears and dried them with her hair. Her great love for me healed her. My precious blood washed you clean. You are no longer sinful, but spotless in my sight. You have been redeemed and forgiven by me. Now go and do likewise to others. Let them know that you hold nothing against them. Show them great love and understanding just as I have done for you.

Lord, please forgive me for all the times that I have sinned against you. Wash me clean and help me never to sin again.

SOWS BOUNTIFULLY

June 16

"Whoever sows sparingly, will also reap sparingly, and whoever sows bountifully will also reap bountifully." 2 Corinthians 9:6

My child, everything you do will have consequences. When you give abundantly to others, they will return the same to you. Even if they do not reciprocate your kindness, your heavenly Father will repay you a hundred fold. So open your heart and give generously to all who ask from you. Not just money, but also your time and your talents. Give with a joyful heart. Whatever you do to the least of your brothers, you do to me.

Loving Father, I thank you for all that you have given to me – your abundant grace and forgiveness. Help me to give generously to all who ask from me.

NO RESISTANCE

June 17

"But I say to you, offer no resistance to one who is evil." Matthew 5:39

Charity or agape is to love not as human beings but as God loves. True charity is when we put others' needs before our own. We love everyone even though the person is not lovable and is full of sin. Love melts all hatred and sinfulness. Love brings about change in another person. Love can move mountains. Learn from me, my child. When they crucified me on the cross, did I resist? When they stripped off my clothes, did I complain? No, I gave it all to save you. As a result of this, people's hearts were turned from evil to good, from hatred to love. Do likewise!

Lord, remove my fear of suffering. Give me the courage to follow your footsteps. Help me to carry my cross daily and increase my love for others.

INNER ROOM

June 18

"But when you pray, go to your inner room, close the door, and pray to your Father in secret." Matthew 6:6

When you pray, visualize me standing right in front of you or next to you. Talk to me as though I am your best friend. Pour out all your heart to me and tell me how you feel. Unless you share your intimate desires with me, we are still only casual friends. Real friendship allows you to bare your soul with another. Do not be afraid to tell me your true feelings. I will understand. I know all that you are going through. Open your mind and your heart to me. I am always waiting for your invitation. Be not afraid to invite me into your heart. Only then will you be able to love others as I love you. Receive my Holy Spirit.

Thank you, my dearest friend and my Savior. Father God, I do want to invite you to come and dwell within me. Holy Spirit, please come!

ELISHA

June 19

"Then Elisha, filled with the twofold portion of his spirit, wrought many marvels by his mere word." Sirach 48:12

My precious child, I chose Elisha to continue the works of Elijah because he was a faithful servant. He left his farming and his family to follow Elijah's footsteps. He was a very humble man. He did not think he could do half the things that Elijah had. That was the reason he asked for a twofold portion. He realized that he needed all the help he could get. His manner was very mild and gentle, not as showy as Elijah. Whosoever is willing to serve me will receive all the necessary gifts of the Holy Spirit. Will you be my disciple and servant? I will always be there for you. I will fill you with my Holy Spirit. You will be able to do wonders and miracles with my help.

Thank you, Lord, for choosing me to be your disciple and servant. Without you I can do nothing. Fill me with the twofold portion of your Spirit.

YOUR EYE

June 20

"The lamp of the body is the eye. If your eye is sound, your whole body will be filled with light; but if your eye is bad, your whole body will be in darkness." Matthew 6:22-23

The spiritual world is as real as this earthly world. Your eyes see all the tangible things around you. But there is treasure hidden in the invisible world. The spiritual world can only be seen by those who are filled with my Spirit. When you are filled with the Holy Spirit you will see what is really important and what is not. The spiritual world is filled with angels and saints. There is only love in their hearts. When your eyes are full of my light you will be able to see love all around you. You will be able to see goodness, kindness, mercy and compassion. Your entire body will be transformed when you are filled with the Holy Spirit. Open your eyes and see what I see.

Lord, I want to see others as you see them. Fill me with your light.

TOMORROW

June 21

"Do not worry about tomorrow; tomorrow will take care of itself. Sufficient for a day is its own evil." Matthew 6:34

My precious child, live each day as if it is your last day on earth for I am always in the present, never in the past or future. I am with you today and every day. I will be with you always. Live each day to the fullest. Never worry about tomorrow. You know that everything you worry about may never happen. It is a waste of your energy and time. Only what you do each day for my honor and glory counts. All other motives are useless. Live each day building my kingdom. Live each day with love and mercy for everyone. Live each day glorifying my Father and pleasing me. The Holy Spirit will be with you each day to strengthen you and to guide you.

I am yours, O Lord. Help me to live each moment for your honor and glory.

ABRAHAM'S DESCENDANT

June 22

"And if you belong to Christ, then you are Abraham's descendant, heirs according to the promise." Galatians 3:29

My child, you are a descendant of Adam and Eve. That is why everyone is related. Everyone is your brother and sister. When you were baptized, you became a part of my family. You have inherited all my relatives and ancestors. You are a part of a royal family, from the line of King David who was a descendant of Abraham. If you only realize who you really are, you will treat everyone very differently. You will love each person like your own relative. You will treasure them like your own family. You will love them as your own flesh and blood. Now go forth and love each one as I have loved you.

Wow! God the Father, you have revealed to me a larger picture of my family line. What an insight. Help me to love everyone as my own sister and brother.

NARROW GATE

June 23

"Enter through the narrow gate; for the gate is wide and the road broad that leads to destruction, and those who enter through it are many." Matthew 7:13

Those who have an easy life usually do not need me. They often forget about me. But those who go through the narrow gate call on me often because they are totally dependent on me. They will not be lost but live an abundant life. They will spend an eternity with me in heaven for they live each day depending totally on me. Their reward will be great. So choose the narrow gate and walk with me always. Carry your cross daily, come and follow me.

Jesus, you are the gate to heaven. I will follow you wherever you lead me.

WONDERFULLY MADE

June 24

"I give you thanks that I am fearfully, wonderfully made." Psalm 139:14

In my vision I saw all different kinds of pieces of a puzzle put together to form an image of Jesus. Jesus said to me, "I love you with an everlasting love. When I created you, I had a purpose for your life in this world - a job only you can do to make my kingdom come true. Every soul is like a piece of the puzzle. Each person is specially designed to fit into my kingdom. Like a piece of the puzzle in your vision, each piece is important to form the whole picture. You are an important part of my creation. You are truly wonderfully made into my image and likeness."

Father God, I praise you for creating me. I want to love you and serve you always.

STOP JUDGING

June 25

"Stop judging, that you may not be judged. For as you judge, so will you be judged." Matthew 7:1

My precious child, every time you judge others you must realize that it is because you are not perfect. In fact, you have the same faults and weaknesses as the person at whom you are pointing your finger. A proud person can spot another person with pride. A talkative person cannot stand another person who likes to talks constantly. A selfish person does not want to be around another self centered person. The list goes on. So, when you see a weakness in another, right away try to improve yourself in that area. Ask me to help you and to see yourself as others see you. Learn from me. I did not come to this world to judge and condemn but to save. Do likewise.

Lord, have mercy on me. Christ, please forgive me for all the times when I have judged others. Help me to be more compassionate and understanding.

YOUR PEARLS

June 26

"Do not give what is holy to dogs, or throw your pearls before swine, lest they trample them underfoot, and turn and tear you to pieces." Matthew 7:6

Share your pearls only with those who are open to receive me. Those are the ones who are ready to accept my words of wisdom. The dogs and the swine are those who come to destroy. They have no intention of being converted. They will not appreciate what you have to offer to them. Their hearts are hardened by sin. They cannot see the truth or change their ways. Give your pearls to those who come to you for help. Only then they will truly appreciate your pearls of wisdom. Only then will they learn from you and try to become holy. Give your pearls to those who are ready to receive me into their hearts. Once they have found me they will be ready to sell everything to get the pearl that I will give them. Are you ready to surrender your life to me?

Lord Jesus, you are the pearl that I treasure. There is no one like you. I want to surrender my life to you.

BE MADE CLEAN

June 27

"He stretched out his hand, touched him and said, 'I will do it. Be made clean.'" Matthew 8: 3

My loving child, I will clean you. I will wash from you all your past sins with my living water. I have already paid the price to heal you on the cross. You are mine. I want to prepare you to enter into my kingdom. Turn your life around. Instead of facing the world, face me. Instead of doing things your way, do my will. Instead of finding faults in everyone around you, see how I have forgiven you. Do likewise to others as I have done for you. The more you are touched by my love and mercy, the more you will be able to love others as I have loved you. Let there be rejoicing in everything you do. From now on, try to do everything according to my will which will bring great joy and honor to my Father. Be cleansed.

Lord, touch me heart so that I might be made clean. Heal me and I shall be healed.

FALSE PROPHETS

June 28

"Beware of false prophets, who come to you in sheep's clothing, but underneath are ravenous wolves." Matthew 7:15

Many people in this world are following false prophets. They do not know the truth. They are like lost sheep following a false prophet wearing sheep's clothing. The false prophets lead others towards death and destruction. Do not be fooled. You will know the prophets who are sent by my Father. They bear good fruit. They live a life sacrificing their own will so as to do my Father's will. They give life and hope to all they meet. They do not come to destroy but to build up my kingdom. They give courage instead of fear. They love instead of hate. They follow all my commandments and do what I ask them to do.

Jesus, lead me to the right prophets. Give me the wisdom and the knowledge to follow only you.

OUR INFIRMITIES

June 29

"He took away our infirmities, and bore our diseases." Matthew 8:17

My precious child, no parents like to see their children suffer from sickness. So, do not be afraid to ask me to heal all your infirmities and diseases. I came into this world to show you that I have power to heal. You, being my child, have the same power to go out and heal people in my name. Do not be afraid to lay hands on people and ask me to heal them. As long as you have me next to you, I will always hear your prayer. All you need to do is to have faith in me. When a person is not healed, maybe it is not time yet. Maybe there are a lot of issues that he needs to work through before he is healed. So do not be afraid to pray for healing. I am the healer and the redeemer.

My God and my Lord, you are truly our healer and our redeemer. In you I trust.

FREEDOM

June 30

"For you are called for freedom. But do not use this freedom as an opportunity for the flesh; rather, serve one another through love." Galatians 5:13

In my vision I saw myself pulling an ox in a muddy field. I was yoked to the ox. It was very hard labor. Then I saw a path, full of light. There was Jesus carrying a cross. I went over to help him. It seemed so easy and light. Jesus said to me, "My precious child, you are set free from your past and your earthly attachments. You are free to follow me. See how my yoke is easy and my burden light. When you follow me, you will be walking in the light. You can see where you are going. It is not suffering, but joy. But when you are tied down to your own desires, you will be dragged down and your burden will be heavy. You will be walking in the mud. Choose me. Choose love above all and you will be set free."

Thank you, Jesus, for showing me the way. Lead me to the right path.

GREAT CALM

July 1

"Then he got up, rebuked the winds and the sea, and there was a great calm." Matthew 8:26

Yes, my precious child I am the Savior of the world. By my words the entire universe was created. All I need to do is say the word. There is power in my word and your words can be just as powerful. So be careful in what you say. Every word you say can have great impact on everyone around you. Your words can bring calmness or chaos. Your words can bring joy and hope to others or hurt and damage to their souls. Your words can build or destroy others. Speak my words whenever you are in trouble. Call on me and I will restore peace and calm around you. Have no fear. Be still and know that I am God.

Lord, you are truly the Almighty God. You are the creator of the entire universe. Even the winds and the seas obey you. I am in awe of your power and glory.

LION'S MOUTH

July 2

"I was rescued from the lion's mouth. The Lord will rescue me from every evil threat and will bring me safely to his heavenly kingdom." 2 Timothy 4:17-18

Do you know, my child, that you are always protected by your guardian angel? Whenever you are out doing my work there will be angels surrounding you and protecting you from all harm. My loving child, do not be afraid or worried about anything. You have me standing by your side always. Wherever I am, a legion of angels will follow. They are there to watch for every evil dart coming your way. They can see the spiritual world as clear as day. They will ward off all that is not from God. They will help you through all difficulties and perils. They will always be at your side. Call on your guardian angel often whenever you are in need of protection.

Thank you my guardian angel for always being there for me. I am grateful for your love and protection.

AUTHORITY

July 3

"When the crowds saw this they were struck with awe and glorified God who had given such authority to human beings." Matthew 9:8

My dear child, sins cripple people like the paralytic. The most common sins are laziness, lack of forgiveness, jealousy and pride. But I came to set you free from your sins, free to love and to serve me. I have authority to drive out all that is crippling you. I have authority over the evil one who is preventing you from living an abundant life, a life full of joy and service to others; a meaningful life that is life giving; a life filled with my purpose for you. The paralytic cannot do anything for others. He is so consumed with his own pain and suffering that he cannot step out and love others. I set him free in front of the crowds. And I can do the same for you, my child.

All praise and glory be yours, my King and my Savior. Thank you for setting me free.

I DESIRE MERCY

July 4

"Go and learn the meaning of the words, 'I desire mercy, not sacrifice.' I did not come to call the righteous but sinners." Matthew 9:13

Mercy comes from your heart. Sacrifice comes from your head. Mercy is filled with love while sacrifice is self-atonement. Mercy is centered upon someone else's feelings and needs. Sacrifice is centered upon one's own sin. It is always far better to love than to say "I am sorry". Love washes away all selfishness and self centeredness. Love heals and rebuilds; sacrifice burns sins away. Love and mercy go hand in hand. I came into the world to show you how to love and to have mercy for all, especially the sinners. Have compassion in your heart. Mercy will follow. Imitate me in all you do. For every loving and merciful act you do you will be greatly rewarded in heaven. Be merciful as my Father is merciful.

Thank you, Jesus, for showing me how to be merciful to all in need. Teach me to love them with compassion.

HOUSEHOLD OF GOD

July 5

"You are no longer strangers and sojourners, but you are fellow citizens with the holy ones and members of the household of God, built upon the foundation of the apostles and prophets, with Christ Jesus himself as the capstone." Ephesians 2:19

Beloved, you are indeed my precious child. I have chosen you to be a part of my family. My Father is your Father too. My mother Mary is your mother. My disciples are all your brothers and sisters. They pray for you constantly. You are protected by angels and you have authority to do the things that I did. You are called and you have a chore to do, just like any member of a family. You are always welcome in our house. You do not need an invitation. My kingdom is your home where you are loved and refreshed. You can be yourself. We have all loved you since the day you were created in your mother's womb.

Jesus, my brother and my best friend, I love you more than anyone on earth. Thank you for making me a part of your holy family.

TREAD UPON SERPENTS

July 6

"Behold, I have given you the power to tread upon serpents and scorpions and upon the full force of the enemy and nothing will harm you." Luke 10:19

In my vision I saw a person stamping bugs under his feet and killing them. Jesus said to me, "If a person is petrified with fear he cannot move his feet and the bugs will start to crawl up his legs and attack him. It is fear that cripples people. Do not be fearful for you know that I am with you always. Conquer all evil by invoking my name. My name has power and no evil can come near you when you speak my name. It is your spiritual weapon. Use it often to ward off all evil. That is why the Our Father prayer is so powerful. Pray, pray and pray."

Glory be to the Father, to the Son and to the Holy Spirit. In the name of Jesus I pray.

ESPOUSE YOU

July 7

"I will espouse you to me forever: I will espouse you in right and in justice, in love and in mercy; I will espouse you in fidelity, and you shall know the Lord." Hosea 2:21-22

In my vision I saw two gold rings. They were linked with each other, inseparable and forever together. Jesus said to me, "My precious darling, the day you were baptized that was the day I chose you to be my spouse. You are the apple of my eye. You are my beloved and my sweetheart. From that day on you were mine. I am with you every moment of the day. Wherever you are, there I will be. We will always be together for eternity for you are precious to me. I have created you in my image and likeness. I have created you with a personality and character that is one of a kind. You are unique. There is no one on earth who can replace you. Come, my love, come to my embrace."

I love you, Lord. My heart sings with joy when I am in your embrace. You are all I want and need.

LABORERS

July 8

"The harvest is abundant but the laborers are few; so ask the master of the harvest to send out laborers for his harvest." Matthew 9:37-38

In my vision I saw a field of grain ready to be cut. At first I saw a person with a long blade swinging and cutting the grain. It was a very slow and tedious job. But then I saw a person sitting on a cutting machine which looked so effortless and easy. Jesus said to me, "When you have the Holy Spirit with you, you are like the person sitting on a machine. Your work will be effortless for my yoke is easy and my burden light. Always invoke the Holy Spirit to help you before you start any job. It will help you in more ways than you can ever imagine. Thank you for saying 'yes' to me. Thank you for being my laborer."

Lord, it is a privilege to work for you. I love praying with people. It gives me so much joy to be of service to you.

LUXURIANT VINE

July 9

"Israel is a luxuriant vine whose fruit matches its growth. The more abundant his fruit, the more altars he built." Hosea 10:1

My precious child, unless the tree is planted by the water it will be dried up and will topple. I am the living water. If you are rooted in me you will bear much fruit. Without me you will fall. You cannot produce any fruit without me. Your works will be all in vain. It will be all for your own pride and glory. A true luxuriant vine is one who listens to me and follows my commandments. Seek my will in all you do. Do not let the enemy rob you of bearing good fruit. Be on guard always. Be alert. Be vigilant. There is a season for everything. Some will bear fruit in the spring, some in the summer and some in the fall. So do not judge others when you see no fruit. It could be they are in their winter season, dormant until next spring. Stay planted next to my living water.

Jesus, you are my true vine and I am your branch. Let me never be separated from you. Help me to bear much fruit.

THE KINGDOM

July 10

"The Kingdom of heaven is at hand. Cure the sick, raise the dead, cleanse the lepers, drive out demons." Matthew 10:7-8

In my vision I saw two kingdoms. In one, the people were all dancing and enjoying each other. There was so much joy and laughter. In the second kingdom, I saw that people were fighting with swords. The people were in pain, fallen on the ground, moaning and screaming. There was so much hatred and revenge. Jesus said to me, "My precious child, the first kingdom you saw is my Kingdom of heaven where love reigns. There are no sick people but all are healthy and well. They enjoy life to the fullest. There is so much joy and celebration. The place where you are living now is the second kingdom that you saw in your vision. There is killing, suffering, doom and gloom. Go now and build my Kingdom here on earth. I will help you in all you do for my Kingdom."

Yes, Lord, I will go with your help. You are our hope and our salvation.

THE MORSEL

July 11

"So he dipped the morsel and took it and handed it to Judas, son of Simon the Iscariot." John 13:26

My child, see how I treated Judas who was about to betray me? Even though I knew what was in his heart, I still treated him with love and compassion. I knew deep down he was trying his best to hasten to build my kingdom. He went alone to do this without first consulting me. He thought he knew better than I. How many times have you gone out and done things without first checking with me? How often have you followed your own ideas and not mine? How many times have you thought you could do it by yourself? The evil one comes in to tempt you as soon as he realizes that you think you can do everything alone. My loving child, do not fall into the trap of this temptation. Never venture out alone for you can do nothing without me. With me all things are possible.

Lord Jesus, please forgive me for all the times that I have not done your will. Help me to remember to lean on you always. I need you more than ever.

BE SHREWD

July 12

"Behold, I am sending you like sheep in the midst of wolves; so be shrewd as serpents and simple as doves." Matthew 10:16

Do not worry about what to say when you pray with people. I will give you the words to speak to their hearts. All you need is to listen to my voice and ask the Holy Spirit to fill you with wisdom and knowledge. Be shrewd as a serpent and simple as a dove. May your "yes" be "yes" and "no" be "no". You do not need to use flowery words. Use my words which will be able to penetrate their hardened hearts. My words have power to separate bone from marrow like a two-edge sword. My words will heal and transform people. Speak my words and pray with my words. They will not come back to you void. I will guide you and prompt you in every situation. Listen to my voice, my love.

Lord, your words are sweeter than honey and more powerful than a two-edged sword. You alone will I listen to. You alone will I serve.

MIGHTY DEED

July 13

"He was not able to perform any mighty deed there, apart from curing a few sick people by laying his hands on them." Mark 6:5

Everyone can lay hands on people and cure them in my name. But to perform mighty deeds one needs to have faith in God Almighty. My relatives and friends at home only saw me as a human being, not divine. They did not have the expectant faith in my divine power. As a result I could not perform any miracles. But you, my precious child, have faith in me and believe in me. With me at your side I will be able to do great things through you. Trust in me and lean on me.

You are my God and my Lord. I do believe that nothing is impossible with you. You are the Son of my Almighty God.

DISCIPLE

July 14

"No disciple is above his teacher, no slave above his master. It is enough for the disciple that he becomes like his teacher, for the slave that he becomes like his master." Matthew 10:24-25

In my vision I saw myself in an exercise class. I followed every move that the teacher did. I breathed in the same manner as the teacher. I followed every step and motion as he was teaching and leading us. Jesus said to me, "My loving child, now you know how to be my true disciple, to follow every action and step that I take. Do not do anything on your own. You might hurt yourself. As long as you imitate me, you will be building your faith and will be able to carry heavier and heavier loads without endangering your body and health. You will build up your muscle and strength and overcome all evil. You will feel more and more joyful as you become more like me. I am your model and your teacher. Come and learn from me. Come and follow me."

O Lord, it is a joy to do your work for you are life giving. You are loving and caring. I want to follow you always.

WHOEVER DENIES ME

July 15

"Whoever denies me before others, I will deny before my heavenly Father." Matthew 10:33

My precious child, see how much joy you have when you speak about your grandsons to others. You are so ready to show his pictures for them to see. That is how I want you to talk about me to others, with love and joy. Let them know what a blessing it is to have me and my Father dwelling in your heart. Tell them all that we have done for you. Tell them the good news about eternal life. Give them the same joy that I have given you. I know you will never deny me but will spread my joy to others.

Lord Jesus, help me to be as eager to share the good news about you with others as I am to share about my grandsons.

THIS COMMAND

July 16

"For this command that I enjoin on you today is not too mysterious and remote for you." Deuteronomy 30:11

Everyone has a loving heart. I have created you to love. You are happiest when you are in love and loved by others. Love gives you meaning in life. Love is what gives you joy. Love is focused on the other person – getting out of selfishness and self centeredness. Love endures all suffering. Love is eternal. When the loved one is absent or void of love, that person is miserable for everyone is created in our image and likeness. To love is to be joyful! To love is to sacrifice and to care for another. To love is to have mercy and compassion. To love is to bring joy to others. My command is written in your heart which is made for love. When you love, you become like me. Your joy will be complete.

I love you, Lord, with my whole heart and soul. Fill me up with more of your love and joy for others.

LIFE

July 17

"Whoever finds his life will lose it, and whoever loses his life for my sake will find it." Matthew 10:39

My loving child, I am the creator of life. When you are following me you are following the way, the truth and the life. Whoever is with me will find abundant life. Every day will be full of joy and meaning. Nothing will be in vain for I am the author of life. It is my breath that sustains you. You cannot function nor have life in you when you are away from me. Stay close to the source of life like a branch grafted to a vine. When you are with me you will bear much fruit, fruit that will last. Without me you can do nothing. But with me you can transform the world. Together we can change lives. Will you give your life for me?

Yes, Lord, I will give you my all. You are the center of my life. In you I find love, peace and joy.

TWO BY TWO

July 18

"Jesus summoned the Twelve and began to send them out two by two and gave them authority over unclean spirits." Mark 6:7

Thank you, my child for your "yes" and your willingness to go wherever I lead you. Do not be concerned about what to say or how to pray. Just invoke the Holy Spirit and he will guide you every step of the way. You need not be afraid of unclean spirits, for you have authority in my name to overcome all spirits. You are my precious child and you have inherited everything from me. Whenever there are two or more of you in my name, there will I be. Go forth and have confidence in me.

Here I am, Lord. I come to do your will. Send your Holy Spirit upon me and guide me in all I do.

CHILDLIKE

July 19

"I give praise to you, Father, Lord of heaven and earth, for although you have hidden these things from the wise and the learned you have revealed them to the childlike." Matthew 11:25

In my vision I saw myself as a little child holding Jesus' hand. We were standing at the edge of the Grand Canyon. He was showing me the sunrise and the sunset, the most beautiful scenery I have ever seen. I was in awe of all the changes of the shapes of the mountains due to the sunlight and the shadows. Jesus said to me, "My love, you are like a little child seeing everything for the first time with my eyes. See the beauty and the splendor of each soul and being as I have first created them. Be in love with everyone. That is the hidden treasure that I give to you today. Each soul is as beautiful as the scenery you saw in your vision. Treasure them."

Jesus, thank you for opening my eyes to see as you see the beauty in each soul. I will try to treasure each person as you have shown me.

HAD NOT REPENTED

July 20

"Jesus began to reproach the towns where most of his mighty deeds had been done, since they had not repented." Matthew 11:20

For those people who do not want to repent for their ways of living even miracles and mighty deeds are useless. They are so set in their ways that they do not want to change. Their hearts are as hardened as stones. They have false idols. They find their security in money, people and things. They want to live each day according to their own will. Their hearts are turned away from me. They have no love for others, only for themselves. They have no time to worship me and to build my kingdom. They do not follow my laws and commands. But you, my child, have repented from your sins and have seen my miracles and mighty deeds. You have turned your life around and have put me first above all else. Continue to make a difference in other people's lives.

Lord, cleanse me of my sins. Wash me, mold me and transform me. I ask forgiveness for all my past sins and I truly have repented them.

MY SOUL

July 21

"My soul yearns for you in the night; yes, my spirit within me keeps vigil for you; when your judgment dawns upon the earth, the world's inhabitants learn justice." Isaiah 26:9

My precious child, I have created you with body, soul, and spirit. Your body will grow old and die, but your soul will live forever. Every soul is precious to me. When I created you, I breathed life into your being. Do not be afraid of those who can harm your body, but fear those who can corrupt your soul. Your soul resides in the center of your being. Without your soul you will have no life in you. Your body is affected by this world, but your soul is affected by the spiritual world. Live each day from the depth of your heart, where your soul resides. To be with me is your soul's greatest desire. Come to me, my beloved child. I yearn for you.

My soul rejoices in you, O Lord. My spirit sings your praises.

MERCY

July 22

"If you knew what this meant, 'I desire mercy, not sacrifice,' you would not have condemned these innocent men." Matthew 12:7

Yes, I am the Divine Mercy. My love for everyone is greater than you can ever imagine. I laid down my life for you even though I knew how painful it would be to die on the cross. There is no greater love than that. My blood covers multitudes of sins. Everyone who eats my body and drinks my blood is saved and will have eternal life. My mercy is for everyone who believes in me and receives me into his heart.

Lord, have mercy on me, a sinner. I thank you for dying on the cross for my sins. Help me to always have mercy towards others.

TREE

July 23

"Every tree is known by its own fruit." Luke 6:44

My child, you are like a palm tree, tall and beautiful. You produce coconut fruit, liquid for drinking and meat that can be used in many products. Every tree produces different fruit. Do not compare yourself with others. The willow tree next to the lake is so beautiful. Its leaves shade people from the hot sun. Some trees are like the cedar in Lebanon. Their wood is the best for building. So you see, I created each one of you different with a special purpose in mind. Do not do what your neighbors are doing. You have a mission in life. I have chosen each one of you, just like the tree with its own kind of leaves and fruits.

God the Father, I treasure all your creation. I thank you for I am wonderfully made. You are an awesome God.

ONLY ONE THING

July 24

"There is need of only one thing. Mary has chosen the better part and it will not be taken from her." Luke 10:42

Everything in this world will pass away. But my word will last forever. Mary chose to listen to my word instead of busying herself in the kitchen like her sister Martha. My word will give you life and purpose while you are living on this earth. My word has true meaning and it will produce much fruit, fruit that will last. Martha was anxious and worried about many things. They were all about earthly matters. Mary knew that only I could bring the eternal word which would put everything into perspective. My word has power to heal and to set people free. My word is the truth, the way and the life. Study my word and ponder it as Mary did. Keep my word in your heart every day of your life.

Lord, give me your word of wisdom, so that I can minister to others better. Your word will lead me to the right path.

BROTHER AND SISTER

July 25

"For whoever does the will of my heavenly Father is my brother, and sister, and mother." Matthew 12:50

My child, you are truly a part of my family. Only today you realized in your heart that you are as special to me as you are to your earthly sisters and brothers. I will never leave you or forsake you. I am always there for you especially in times of your need. Remember when you were sick, your sisters and brothers were so concerned about you. They sent you the biggest bouquet of roses. When you were moving, some of your brothers and sisters came to help you move into your new place. You can trust in me more than your siblings for I am your God and your provider. I will always hold you in the palm of my hand. Continue to spend each day with me. You will have joy in doing my will.

Thank you, Jesus, for being my brother. I am overjoyed to know that I am a part of your family. I feel so blessed.

RESURRECTION

July 26

"I am the resurrection and the life; whoever believes in me, even if he dies, will live, and anyone who lives and believes in me will never die. Do you believe this?" John 11:25-26

In my vision I saw myself holding onto a helium balloon, which was going up and up into the sky. Jesus said to me, "My precious child, in the same way whoever holds on to me and believes in me will go up and up into heaven where there is no death or sorrow. Heaven is pure love and pure joy. Love lives on forever. Sin leads to death. Choose love always. As long as you are holding onto me, you will be saved. Alone you can never reach heaven. It is not by your own deeds that you will get there, but by doing God's will which will enrich your life. Life without me is empty and meaningless. Choose me above all. Choose me in every decision you make. Choose love."

Lord, you are my life and my salvation. I choose to live each day for you. Jesus, I want to be with you forever.

GET SUCH WISDOM

July 27

"Where did this man get such wisdom and mighty deeds?" Matthew 13:54

My child, all wisdom comes from God. Without wisdom a person walks in the dark. He does not know where he is coming and going. With wisdom he is able to see clearly the reality of life. It is like a person holding onto a bright flashlight. He knows exactly where he is going and where he has been. I am the light of the world. I am the seed of wisdom. Whoever follows me will have the wisdom to make the right choices and decisions. Without my wisdom you will stumble and fall. You cannot make wise choices alone that will lead you into my kingdom. Like Solomon, pray for wisdom. Ask the Holy Spirit to fill you with his wisdom and knowledge.

Come, Holy Spirit. Fill me with your wisdom and truth. Help me to walk in your light.

THE LOAVES

July 28

"Then Jesus took the loaves, gave thanks, and distributed them to those who were reclining, and also as much of the fish as they wanted." John 6:11

My loving child, if you give away from what you have to those who are in need, I will be able to multiply these gifts and to perform miracles. Give whatever you can and leave the result to me for nothing is impossible with God. All I want from you is your willingness to share and to do my will. Leave the rest to me. You just do what I ask you and the rest will be taken care of by me. Share generously with all who ask from you. Your reward will be great in heaven.

Lord, give me a generous heart. You are the miracle worker. You are the Son of God.

PARABLES

July 29

"I will open my mouth in parables, I will announce what has lain hidden from the foundation of the world." Matthew 13:35

A parable, my child, is one of the ways that I can teach you about the deep truth of the mysteries of life. It describes the spiritual world in comparison to the material world. It simplifies the theological truth of everyday living in a manner you will be able to understand. A good example is the parable of the mustard seed compared to the kingdom of God. The smallest seed will grow into a large bush. So it will be in my kingdom.

Lord, I love to read the stories that you told us from the Bible. You have the words of everlasting life.

WEEDS

July 30

"Just as the weeds are collected now and burned up with fire, so will it be at the end of the age." Matthew 13:40

My loving child, when you see a weed in your yard you quickly pull it out because if you do not do it while the weed is small it will be difficult to pull it out when it is big. So it is with sin. It is easier to change your ways as soon as you see yourself doing something wrong than to wait until later. The longer you hold onto sin the harder it is to correct it. So weed often. Go to reconciliation as often as you can. I will give you the grace to overcome your sins. I will wash you clean with my living water.

Jesus, I am heartily sorry for my sins. Please help me to change my ways.

WASHED YOUR FEET

July 31

"If I, therefore, the master and teacher, have washed your feet, you ought to wash one another's feet. I have given you a model to follow, so that as I have done for you, you should also do." John 13:14-15

Do you think I could wash my disciples' feet standing up? No, of course not. I had to kneel down to unfasten their sandals. I did this to show you how to do likewise to all those who need my love and care. Peter said to me, "You will never wash my feet," because he realized how sinful and weak a person he was. Peter was my favorite disciple because he was so honest and he loved me so deeply. He wanted to serve me and to wash my feet. Would you let me wash your feet? Would you let me see all your imperfections and sins? Would you be humble enough to let me unfasten your sandals? Surrender yourself into my care. Let me wash your feet so that you too can be my disciple.

Lord, I am not worthy that you kneel down before me and wash my feet. Give me the humility to do the same to all those who are in need of your love.

TREASURE

August 1

"Thus will it be for all who store up treasure for themselves but are not rich in what matters to God." Luke 12:21

My precious child, gold is valueless in heaven. In fact, the walkway in heaven is paved with gold. It is something everybody walks on. It is people's souls that are treasures in heaven. Each soul is priceless for I have created each human being in my image and likeness. Every time you choose people above money or gold you are storing treasures and riches in heaven. Money and gold only lead to greed and discontent. The love of people is priceless. Love is what I treasure. I created each one with a heart capable of loving me and others. But many people have turned away from me and crave only material goods. My child, go and help them to store up riches in heaven. Help them to turn their hearts back to me.

You are my treasure and my all, O Lord. I love you with all my soul, with all my strength and with all my heart.

MEEKEST MAN

August 2

"Moses himself was by far the meekest man on the face of the earth." Numbers 12:3

Meekness is obedience to God. When you depend totally upon my Father in everything you do and say then you will become like Moses in his meekness. Moses left the good life in the desert with his family when God called him to go back to Egypt to set the slaves free. He obeyed God even though he did not think he was qualified to do such a big job. He laid down his life for others. He suffered forty years in the desert leading the slaves out of Egypt. He was the meekest man in God's eyes. My child, go and do my Father's will.

Lord, give me the meekness and the courage to step out and follow my calling. Help me to embrace all that you have planned for me to do.

A VOICE

August 3

"Then from the cloud came a voice that said, 'This is my chosen Son; listen to him.'" Luke 9:35

My loving child, you can only hear my voice when you are not talking or doing too many things. To listen effectively you need to be quiet and ready to receive. You cannot listen to my voice if there is constant chattering and noise. The quieter you are, the more you will be able to hear me. My voice is a soft and whispering voice. I speak to your heart. If your heart is hard as a rock you will not be able to receive my message. If your mind is thinking of too many other things I will not be able to communicate with you. If you are rushing around with too many chores you will miss my voice and my presence. Be still and know that I am your God. I long to talk to you. Listen to my voice.

Speak to me, Lord; your servant is listening. Here I am, Lord, ready to do your will.

HAVE ME

August 4

"You always have the poor with you, but you do not always have me." John 12:8

Yes, the poor will always be there but every moment you spend alone with me is more precious than all the work and money you give to the poor. Without an intimate relationship with me you will be doing all the good deeds for your own glory and pleasure. That is why the saints spend many hours praying and communing with me every day. It is not how much work you perform that will make you a saint. It is how much you really love me. All my mother did was household chores everyday while I was growing up. But her love for me was more than anyone else's love on earth. Her eyes were always upon me. We were together for 30 years. She held me; she cooked for me and she took care of me. There is no one who loves me more than my mother. Imitate her, my loving child. Ask her to intercede for you daily. She is your mother too.

Mary, my mother, please pray for me that I will be able to love your son Jesus more and more each day. Help me to grow closer to him daily.

CHEERFUL GIVER

August 5

"Each must do as already determined, without sadness or compulsion, for God loves a cheerful giver." 2 Corinthians 9:7

In my vision I saw a little girl dressed like a flower girl in a wedding. She had a basket of rose petals in her hand. She was spreading the petals everywhere she went. She was walking in front of the bride. Jesus said to me, "My precious child, if you want to please me, do the same as the little flower girl in your vision. Spread the good news, which is like the rose petals, everywhere you go. Bring my fragrance and joy to all you meet. Be my servant in giving blessings to others. You are my hands and my feet now. You are my generous giver. You are my ambassador to the world. Let everyone who sees you, sees me. I am walking in front of you. You are my joy."

Yes, Lord Jesus, I want to spread your joy and love to everyone I meet today. Show me the way.

TWO OF YOU

August 6

"If two of you agree on earth about anything for which they are to pray, it shall be granted to them by my heavenly Father." Matthew 18:19

My precious child, my heavenly Father loves all his children. When two of you ask anything in my name he cannot refuse. He knows that your petition is for the good of others. He is a generous and loving Father. He wants to bless his children as much as you want to pray for others. His heart is softened when he hears you praying in unison with others. When you pray with love in your heart he cannot refuse you. He hears your petitions. He knows your needs. He has a compassionate heart that wants to heal all those who ask for healing. He hears your prayers. So do not be afraid to ask for anything in my name. It is our will that your prayers are heard. It is our joy to hear you pray together.

Lord God, you are more loving and generous than we can ever imagine. Thank you for always answering our prayers.

ON A CROSS

August 7

"He humbled himself, becoming obedient to the point of death, even death on a cross." Philippians 2:8

Do you have any idea the pain I suffered for you on the cross? Each nail not only pierced my hands and feet, but also my heart. My heart ached more than any part of my body. I felt totally abandoned and deserted by everyone, even my loving Father in heaven, because I took on all the sins of the world. Every sin separates us from our Father. That was one of the most painful moments for me on the cross. My disciples all ran away from me except John. Peter, who had denied me three times, was nowhere in sight. Only my mother Mary and a few of my favorite women disciples remained with me till the end. My beloved child, look at me on the cross and meditate on how much I love you. Let your tears flow. Wash my pierced feet with them and wipe my bloody feet with your hair. I love you more than you will ever know.

My loving Jesus, it breaks my heart for me to see you on the cross. I will never be able to do for you for what you have done for me. I love you, Jesus.

ONE FLESH

August 8

"For this reason a man shall leave his father and mother and be joined to his wife, and the two shall become one flesh." Matthew 19:5

My child, I created male and female so that they complement each other. They fulfill each other's needs. After marriage they truly become one flesh. This union is bound with love. This marriage will only work when they are willing to lay down their lives for one another. It is with love for each other that children are conceived. Those who are united with me will bear much fruit like the married couple. It is through this union that love is perfected. Love can conquer all evil. Love unites and brings joy and happiness. No sacrifice is too much when there is true love and true union.

Lord, I thank you and praise you for creating me to love you and every creature in this universe. I thank you for blessing me with a loving spouse, children and grandchildren.

I WILL DELIVER

August 9

"I will deliver them from all their sins of apostasy, and cleanse them so that they may be my people and I will be their God." Ezekiel 37:23

In my vision I saw Jesus opening the prison doors and letting the prisoners go free. They all followed him out the door. Jesus said to me, "It is my greatest desire to deliver my people from their sins and false idols, for they do not know what they are doing. Can statues or idols save your soul? Can they rescue you from danger? Can they comfort you when you are broken-hearted and sad? My loving child, I will be there for you whenever you call on me. I am your God and your redeemer. I will set you free from all your misery. You are no longer locked in your past sins no matter how great or small they were. You are set free. Free to worship me. Free to call on me and lean on me. I will carry you on eagle's wings and bring you to my Father's house."

What freedom! What joy! Thank you, Jesus, for setting me free from all my past sins. Alleluia! Praise the Lord.

CHILDREN

August 10

"Let the children come to me, and do not prevent them; for the kingdom of heaven belongs to such as these." Matthew 19:14

Come, my precious child, let me bless you. Everyone on earth is my child. I love all my children. Bring everyone closer to me so that I can bless them too. See how much you love your children and only want the best for them? Now you can imagine how much more I love each one of you. There is no greater love than the one who lays down his life for you. I will do anything for you. Come to me and spend intimate and quality time alone with me. My greatest joy is to be with each one of my children with a time to share and a time to listen from heart to heart. So come often and sit by me. I will bless you and fill you with my love and grace.

Here I am, Lord. Speak, Lord. Your child is listening.

STORMS AND DANGERS

August 11

"I called out: O Lord, you are my father, you are my champion and my savior; do not abandon me in time of trouble, in the midst of storms and dangers." Sirach 51:10

In my vision I saw a hurricane destroying all the houses and cars except for one little house which was still standing in perfect condition. Jesus said to me, "My child, you see I am the Lord of wind and rain. Even the storm listens to me. That little house you saw in your vision is one who is protected by me from all harm. You are my precious child. I heard your cry and I came to rescue you. Even though everything seems hopeless you will not be harmed or destroyed. My loving arms wrap around you and protect you from all enemies. They will not be able to go near you because they are afraid of me. Remember this vision always whenever you are in trouble. I am with you till the end of time. Have no fear whatsoever, my love."

My God and my Lord, in you I trust with my whole being. You are my rock and my salvation.

ABRAM PROSTRATED HIMSELF

August 12

"When Abram prostrated himself, God spoke to him, 'My covenant with you is this: you are to become the father of a host of nations.'" Genesis 17:3

Do you know, my child, why I chose Abram to be the father of many nations? It is because he listened to and worshiped me. He was obedient to me and followed my commandments. He trusted me when I told him to leave his land and hometown and go to a place he had never been before. He put me above all things and people. He was willing to sacrifice his son on the altar for me. Such faithfulness, such obedience is what I seek in each person. You, my child, have been chosen too. Are you willing to leave everything and follow me? Are you willing to sacrifice your own son for me? Will you follow me and go wherever I go? Are you ready to say "yes" to me? I will bless you abundantly as I have blessed Abram.

Lord, give me the courage and the faith to follow you, no matter where you are leading me. I want to give you my life for you are my God and my redeemer.

SLAVE OF SIN

August 13

"Amen, amen, I say to you, everyone who commits sin is a slave of sin." John 8:34

In my vision I saw two small children, like Hansel and Gretel, holding hands and finding candies on the ground and eating them as they walked towards the witch's house. Jesus said to me, "Sin is turning away from me and searching for self gratification. It leads to slavery and death. Most people do not realize how many temptations there are in this world. Beware, my precious child. Do not follow the world, but come and follow me. The minute you find yourself not looking at me notice what your eyes are searching. If it is not pure and holy turn around immediately and refocus on me. The wage of sin is death. If you only knew how much I have suffered for your sins you would never sin again."

Lord Jesus, please forgive me for all the times when I have wandered far away from you. I pray that I will stay close to you always.

YOU KNOW ME

August 14

"So Jesus cried out in the temple area as he was teaching and said, 'You know me and also know where I am from.'" John 7:28

My precious child, you do know me when you are in church or during your prayer time. But when you are outside church, do you see me in other people's faces? Do you know where they are from? If you knew, you would love each one as much as you love me for I am in each soul. I know where they come from. Some people go through a lot in their lives and they need understanding and compassion. Some have suffered much and need comfort and mercy. Some have never been loved and are craving for love. Will you be my hands and my heart to them? Will you hold them in your arms for me? Every time you do good deeds to the least of my people you are doing them to me. My Father will reward you a hundredfold. Look for me when you are out and about. You will know me when you take the time to see me everywhere you go.

Lord, open my eyes to see you in every soul I meet today. Send your Holy Spirit upon me so that I will be able to love everyone, especially those who most need your love.

MARY

August 15

"Mary set out and travelled to the hill country in haste to a town of Judah, where she entered the house of Zechariah and greeted Elizabeth." Luke 1:39-40

Mary was chosen to be my mother because of her total trust in my Father. She was filled with the Holy Spirit the moment she said "yes" to the angel Gabriel. She set out in haste to Elizabeth's house because she believed what the angel told her about her cousin's pregnancy in her old age. She believed that nothing is impossible with God. With me in her womb she brought joy to Elizabeth and baby John. She brought reassurance to her cousin that all would go well. When you welcome Mary as your mother, you welcome me also in your heart. We go forth together to bring joy to everyone who welcomes us. Mary my mother was assumed into heaven, but she and I are always with you. You are our precious child.

Hail Mary, full of grace. The Lord is with you. Blessed are you among women. Blessed is the fruit of your womb, Jesus.

WITHOUT SIN

August 16

"Let the one among you who is without sin be the first to throw a stone at her." John 8:7

My loving child, everyone has sinned since the fall of Adam and Eve. Everyone has turned away from God. That is the reason I had to die on the cross to redeem you from your sin. I paid the price with my blood. There is no other suffering more painful than a slow agonizing death on the cross. I washed you clean with water and blood that came from my side. You are mine. No one can take you away from me. We are chained together by my love. We are linked with each other forever. Keep your face looking up into heaven. Focus on my loving Father, not on the problems of this world. Live in my kingdom. Live without sin. Shine your love and joy on all you meet today. Treat everyone with respect and compassion.

Wash me clean with your precious blood, O Lord. Help me to avoid all temptations. Give me the courage to follow you always.

A HUNDRED TIMES

August 17

"Everyone who has given up houses or brothers or sisters or father or mother or children or lands for the sake of my name will receive a hundred times more, and will inherit eternal life." Matthew 19:29

It is like the multiplication of loaves and fishes. Whatever you offer to others for my sake I can multiply a hundred times more. Give away whatever you have in my name's sake and I can transform that into the salvation of many. It is not due to your own efforts but with me all things are possible. So do not be afraid to sacrifice and to give what is dear to you. Your reward will be great in heaven. You will inherit eternal life with me. You will enjoy eternal bliss and joy with me. You will be rewarded a hundred times more. Come, my loving child.

Lord, give me a generous heart so that I will be willing to give up all for your name's sake. I want to serve you till the end of my life.

MOLTEN CALF

August 18

"They have soon turned aside from the way I pointed out to them, making for themselves a molten calf and worshiping it, sacrificing to it and crying out, 'This is your God, O Israel, who brought you out of the land of Egypt!'" Exodus 32:8

In my vision I saw a golden calf in the middle of a crowd of people where they were all singing, dancing and having their orgies. Jesus said to me, "My child, my heart is heavy with sorrow with the world situation today. People have turned away from me. They no longer worship me or listen to me. Instead, they have created for themselves false gods. Their lives are centered on materialism and instant self gratification. But you, my precious child, have been faithful to me. Continue to receive my body and blood and to read the scriptures daily. They will nourish you and strengthen you as protection from all the evil around you. Pray without ceasing for the people in this world, especially for your country, all your family members and friends. Pray, pray and pray."

My God and my Lord, please forgive us for all the times when we have not worshiped you or adored you. Please turn our hearts back to you, Lord.

RESURRECTION OF LIFE

August 19

"Do not be amazed at this, because the hour is coming in which all who are in the tombs will hear his voice and will come out, those who have done good deeds to the resurrection of life, but those who have done wicked deeds to the resurrection of condemnation." John 5:28

My loving child, while I was on earth I did everything that my Father wished me to do. I did not do anything according to my own will but only according to my Father's will. So it is with you. When you do good deeds for my Father's honor and glory you will have resurrection of life. You will enjoy the heavenly banquet with us one day. You will spend eternity without tears and sorrow. The time is coming soon when you can no longer do any good deeds for others. Do not waste a moment being idle. Go out and carry out my mission to heal the sick, set the captives free and proclaim the good news to the poor.

My loving Father, here I am ready to do your will. Help me to focus my eyes upon you and to do whatever you have planned for me to do today.

WEDDING GARMENT

August 20

"My friend, how is it that you came in here without a wedding garment? But he was reduced to silence." Matthew 22:12

My precious child, everyone is given an opportunity to put on a wedding garment before they enter into my kingdom of heaven. The wedding garment is your baptism gown and all your righteousness and good deeds. Everyone has a lifetime to do good work and to be righteous. Those who are lazy and waste their time in pursuing things of this world instead of following my statutes and commandments will come to my wedding feast unprepared and empty handed. They will be bound and thrown into the darkness outside of heaven. Only those who are prepared for the wedding feast like the wise bridesmaids with oil in their lamps will be able to enjoy the banquet with me. Be watchful, be prepared and be diligent.

Lord, I long for the day to enjoy the wedding banquet which you have prepared for me. Help me to be ready and to stay faithful to you till the end.

VISION

August 21

"One night while Paul was in Corinth, the Lord said to him in a vision, 'Do not be afraid. Go on speaking, and do not be silent, for I am with you.'" Acts 18:9

In my vision I saw Jesus and myself riding on a bicycle for two. He was in the front and I sat behind him. We both were pedaling. Jesus said to me, "My child, when you are with me, I will take you places where you have never been. Have no fear. You will enjoy the scenery without a care in the world. It will be a total bliss. But you need to do your part. As in your vision which I gave you, you were not idle sitting behind me but pedaling as we went along. I need your input and your help. With me in the front, you will not have any worry. You can place your trust in me and know that nothing will harm you or hurt you. Enjoy the ride. Enjoy each day. I am with you always."

Lord Jesus, what a beautiful vision. I thank you for being always with me. Help me to trust you more and more each day.

HUMBLES HIMSELF

August 22

"Whoever exalts himself will be humbled; but whoever humbles himself will be exalted." Matthew 23:12

My child, to be humble is to always think others better than yourself. Do not feel that you have all the answers or that you are the only one who can do the job. A humble person listens to others and is willing to change and to admit when he is wrong. A humble person depends totally on God and knows that everything comes from above. When you feel you can do it all by yourself you have become proud like the Pharisees. Do not do things to show off or to seek high places for your own glory. Learn from me, for I am meek and humble at heart. Love and honor each person because everyone has value and is precious in my sight. True humility is seen in the person who knows his own weaknesses and strength. Be humble at heart.

Thank you, Lord, for showing me how to be humble and meek. May everything I do give you honor and glory.

BLIND FOOLS

August 23

"Blind fools, which is greater, the gold, or the temple that made the gold sacred?" Matthew 23:17

Choose me, my precious child, above all your earthly possessions. Gold will devalue but my love for you is priceless. Do not be like those who are blinded by their riches. They like to think that life is all about money. But you know better, my love. Your life without me will be totally empty. It will be worthless. There are two paths in life you can walk. One is to follow riches and the other is to follow me. With me, you will reach heaven and enter into my kingdom. With riches, you will be led to destruction and death. You can serve either gold or God. Choose me above all else. I am your wealth and your inheritance. I am all you need.

Lord, you are more precious than gold or silver. I will always choose you above everything else.

TWELVE GATES

August 24

"It had a massive, high wall, with twelve gates where twelve angels were stationed and on which names were inscribed, the names of the twelve tribes of the children of Israel." Revelation 21:12

My precious child, I have prepared a place in heaven for you and your family - a place which eyes have not seen and ears have not heard the splendor of the new Jerusalem. You are my bride. I have paid the price for you on the cross already. You are mine. Your family is my family. Your friends are my friends. All the people you treasure here on earth are precious to me too. Come and enjoy the feast that I have prepared for you. You will not be disappointed. There will be laughter and music. There will be love and peace forever. Come, my beloved.

Glory and praise to you, my Lord and my God. I look forward to the day when I will join you in heaven.

WHITE WASHED TOMBS

August 25

"Woe to you, scribes and Pharisees, you hypocrites. You are like white washed tombs, which appear beautiful on the outside, but inside are full of dead men's bones and every kind of filth." Matthew 23:27

My dear child, be transparent. Be honest and truthful. Be my imitator. People will see you and know you when you are sincere with them. Do not hide any of your actions – good or bad. Be humble. Guard your mouth before you speak. Your speech should be loving and caring. This way your conscience will be clear. Be simple like Mother Teresa. Do what is right, not for show, but do every action to please me. Let that be your only motive. Let every word you speak give me glory. Let every action you do be in my name. Only in this way will you be clean from inside out.

Heavenly Father, I only want to please you in everything I do and say. Help me to be truthful and honest in all my motives.

STAY AWAKE

August 26

"Stay awake! For you do not know on which day your Lord will come." Matthew 24:42

Keep your eyes open and focus upon me, my child. When you have your eyes closed, you will trip and fall. Stay awake and stay alert. Only then will you be able to see the spiritual world which is as real as the physical world around you. Most people go through life with their eyes half open. They do not have expectant faith in me. They live each day without a purpose for their lives. But you, my precious child, live each moment for the greater glory of God. Let every word you speak bring others closer to me. Let every action be filled with love and compassion for others. Be generous with your time, praying for others. Be vigilant and you will realize that I am with you. With me at your side, you will be able to live each day to the fullest, all for the honor and glory of my Father. Live each day doing good deeds without any anxiety or stress. Live in the present moment. Watch for me and wait for me as when you were waiting for your loved one to come home. Wait with great joy and excitement.

Lord, my heart longs to be with you. I look forward to the day when I can see you face to face. You are my love and my treasure.

ETERNAL ROCK

August 27

"Trust in the Lord forever! For the Lord is an eternal rock." Isaiah 26:4

In my vision I saw a golden temple built on a huge solid rock. Jesus said to me, "My child, I am the eternal rock. I will never change nor waver. I will always stand firm on every word I speak. You can trust me and lean on me. I am the way, the truth and the life. There is no other God besides me. Climb on my rock and come to me. I will shelter you in times of distress. I will protect you from all harm. I will shield you from the evil one. You are mine. Come to my temple and worship me day and night. I hear all your prayers and petitions. I will answer you and grant your wishes. Trust me as a child trusts his parents. You have no worries about anything, but hold fast unto me. I am your rock and your salvation."

My Lord and my God, in you alone I trust. You are my rock and my salvation. There is no other.

FAITHFUL SERVANT

August 28

"Well done, my good and faithful servant. Since you were faithful in small matters, I will give you great responsibilities. Come, share your master's joy." Matthew 25:21

I know what you are capable of doing, my child. I will never ask you to do more than you can manage. In the parable, the person who had 5 talents went and traded. He made 5 more. The person who was given only 2 talents, made 2 more. Both made the master very happy. Both were rewarded with greater responsibility. But the one with only one talent was afraid to lose it and he buried it instead of investing it. Do not be afraid to use all the gifts that I have given to you. The more you use them, the better servant you will be. Be fruitful. Go and share your talents with others. The more you have the more will be given to you. Be my joyful and faithful servant.

Lord, I want to be your good and faithful servant. Remove any fear that might prevent me from serving you in every situation of my life.

EYES WERE UNDIMMED

August 29

"Moses was 120 years old when he died, yet his eyes were undimmed and his vigor unabated." Deuteronomy 34:7

Do not be fearful of old age, my precious child. If you continue to serve me and to obey me, you shall have a healthy and happy life even in your senior years. You will experience peace in all circumstances if you stay close to me and abide in me. With me, you will have no fear, anxiety or stress. Without me, you will have to struggle each day of your life. I am your good shepherd. I will protect you with my rod and staff. Rejoice always and be glad.

Gracious God, I thank you and praise you for my life. Everything I have comes from you. You are my good shepherd.

SPIRIT AND LIFE

August 30

"The words I have spoken to you are Spirit and life." John 6:63

In my vision I saw God's word like a butterfly. It flies wherever it wants to go and it pollinates whatever it touches. It bears much fruit. It is always moving and it is so beautiful. Jesus said to me, "Yes, my child, my word has power. It gives life wherever it touches. The Spirit moves wherever it wills. It is like a breath of fresh air. It renews and refreshes the soul. Spend quality time with my scriptures every day of your life. It will enrich your life and fill you with wisdom."

Lord Jesus, fill me with your word, which is more precious than silver or gold. You word is my guiding light.

DELIGHT

August 31

"For I create Jerusalem to be a joy and its people to be a delight; I will rejoice in Jerusalem and exult my people." Isaiah 65:18

My precious child, do you remember the set of beautiful jade animals that your father had years ago? He used to take them out often from a secret compartment in his desk and admire them. Those animals were his treasures for many years. You are my treasure and my delight. My eyes are always upon you. I will store you in my heart so no enemy can snatch you away from me. Every movement you make and every word you say are important to me, for I have created you in your mother's womb. There is no one like you in the entire universe. You are unique. You are my priceless gem. I have paid for you with my own flesh and blood. I want you to be with me for eternity. You are my beloved and I am yours.

I love you, Lord, with my whole heart, whole soul and my entire being. Take me into your heart and never let me be separated from you. I am all yours.

THE WIND CEASED

September 1

"He woke up, rebuked the wind, and said to the sea, 'Quiet! Be still!' The wind ceased and there was a great calm." Mark 4:39

Yes, my words have power. Even the wind and the storm obey me. Your words have power too. Your words can build or hurt another person. Your words can encourage or put fear into people's hearts. Your words can heal or destroy another person. So use your words wisely. Do not say anything that is hurtful or not loving. You can never take your words back. Once they are spoken, there is no turning back. My loving child, always think before you speak.

Lord, please guard my lips. Help me to use my words wisely, according to your will.

HOLY MOUNTAIN

September 2

"There shall be no harm or ruin on my holy mountain; for the earth shall be filled with knowledge of the Lord, as water covers the sea." Isaiah 11:9

In my vision I saw a large mountain topped with snow, like Mt. Fuji. As I started to climb the mountain at the beginning it was easy because it was not too steep. As I went further and further up the terrain became full of rocks and snow. It was very difficult and cold. Finally when I reached the top of the mountain the view all around me was breath-taking. I saw a large eagle fly by. It must have been the Holy Spirit who guided me all along even though I did not know he was there until I got to the top. It was at that moment I could see the world from God's point of view. It was so peaceful and everything looked so beautiful. I knew that I got there only because I followed Jesus who went ahead of me. I could never have done it alone.

Thank you, God, for this beautiful vision. I shall always treasure it. You are an awesome God!

HE REBUKED THEM

September 3

"He rebuked them and did not allow them to speak because they knew that he was the Messiah." Luke 4:41

Head knowledge is not the same as heart knowledge, my child. Knowing me is not the same as worshiping me. The demons know who I am but they refuse to worship me. That is why I rebuked them. You are my child; you know me and you love me. I will never rebuke you nor stop you from speaking the good news to others. You honor me by your good deeds. You bring others to me. You are my precious child in whom I am well pleased.

Lord, I love you with all my heart. Protect me from all the evil ones. Help me to proclaim your good news to everyone.

CATCHING MEN

September 4

"Do not be afraid; from now on you will be catching men."
Luke 5:10

My precious child, if you do everything that I tell you, you too will be awed by the results of your work as were my disciples Peter and John. For I have a plan to build my kingdom on earth. I know when is a good time for you to lower your net in order to get a good catch. I know the best place for you to catch men. If you only learn to listen and to follow my guidance every project you do for me will bring many souls to me. It is my greatest desire that you and all my disciples enjoy the wedding feast with me in my kingdom. Come, my faithful servant.

Here I am, Lord. I come to do your will. May your kingdom come!

WITHOUT BLEMISH

September 5

"God has now reconciled you in the fleshly Body of Christ through his death, to present you holy, without blemish, and irreproachable before him." Colossians 1:22

Keep yourself pure and sinless, my child. Put on Christ. Imagine yourself dressed in this radiant white garment that I gave to you on the day of your baptism. Keep it unblemished always. Learn to live a life without hatred or resentment. Fill yourself with the light of Christ for you have been washed by the water and the blood of Christ. You have been ransomed from the slavery of sin. So now go and live a life that radiates Christ, a life full of love and joy.

Lord, let me spread your love to others. Help me to put on Christ. Keep me pure and unblemished.

UNLEAVENED BREAD

September 6

"Therefore let us celebrate the feast, not with the old yeast, the yeast of malice and wickedness, but with the unleavened bread of sincerity and truth." 1 Corinthians 5:8

My loving child, be my unleavened bread. Be without puffed up pride in all you do for me. Let every word and deed be truthful and sincere. Only then will you be truly pleasing to me. Let your motive be pure and simple. Focus every job you do for me with joy. I love a cheerful giver. A joyful heart is a sincere heart. Do everything in my name. Do everything with love in your heart. Do everything without expecting any reward from others. Your Father sees every deed you do and he will reward you a hundredfold. He knows what is in your heart. He knows your motives and good intentions. He sees the truth. So be not afraid to step out and do good to others. I am with you always.

Lord Jesus, it is a joy and a delight to work for you every day. You are my strength and my purpose in life.

HE WAS PIERCED

September 7

"But he was pierced for our offenses, crushed for our sins, upon him was the chastisement that makes us whole, by his stripes we were healed." Isaiah 53:5

In my vision I saw a soldier pounding a large nail into Jesus' hand. With every strike, my heart ached and I covered my eyes which were filled with tears and sorrow. Jesus said to me, "My child, do not cry for me. Cry for your sins. Every sin causes me as much pain as this nail which was pierced into me. I love you and I willingly suffer for you so that one day you will be set free and join me in heaven where you will have no more tears or sorrow. That is why I said, 'If you love me you will keep my commandments.' Everyone who does not keep my commandments has sinned against my Father. When you keep my commandments, you will be set free and you will have a life full of freedom and joy."

Lord Jesus, thank you for all the suffering that you have endured for my sake. I love you with my whole heart. I am heartily sorry for all my sins.

HOLY SPIRIT

September 8

"For it is through the Holy Spirit that this child has been conceived in her." Matthew 1:20

My precious child, you have the Holy Spirit too. You can also say "Yes" like my mother Mary and carry me in your heart. Every time you bring me to others you bring hope and joy to them. Every time you let me use you, you become my faithful servant. The Holy Spirit dwells in you and will prompt you to do everything with great love. Every little act will be for my honor and glory. Imitate my mother Mary. She is a perfect model for you.

I love you, Jesus, Mary and Joseph. Be with me today and every day. Come, Holy Spirit, and fill my heart with your love.

EARTHLY

September 9

"Put to death, then, the parts of you that are earthly: immorality, impurity, passion, evil desires, and the greed that is idolatry." Colossians 3:5

In my vision I saw myself climbing a rocky mountain. The more things I carried, the harder it was for me to climb to the top. Jesus said to me, "My child, this is what happens when you are attached to earthly things and sinful desires. They will drag you down. They will distract you from reaching your goal which is eternal life with me. What joy we will have when you finally reach the top. I will help you along the way, but, I cannot get rid of your baggage for you. You must be willing to discard it yourself. Unload all your attachments; come and follow me."

Lord, I can hardly wait to be with you for eternity. Help me to empty myself so that I will be able to reach you at the top of the mountain.

LOVE YOUR ENEMIES

September 10

"Love your enemies, do good to those who hate you, bless those who curse you, pray for those who mistreat you." Luke 6:27-28

My child, your enemies are my children too. The only way to treat your enemies is to love them as I have loved them. I died on the cross for everyone, Jews, Gentiles, Muslims, pagans and all. So, have no hatred for anyone. Only love will bring about their conversion. Only love heals and unites all. It is my greatest desire that all may be one as my Father and I are one. So go and love, love and love. Love even your enemies.

Lord Jesus, give me a big heart like yours, so that I will be able to love everyone. Help me to be more compassionate and merciful.

IN HIS IMAGE

September 11

"God created man in his image; in the divine image he created him; male and female he created them." Genesis 1:27

Look in the mirror, my precious child. What do you see? I see a beautiful soul created in my image and likeness. I see a soul capable of loving others, even those you do not know. I see a soul ready to forgive and to repent. All the qualities that Jesus mentioned on the Mount of Beatitudes are the qualities of a soul. With me you can be a peacemaker, a merciful and joyful person, a person full of gratitude willing to lay down your life for me and for others. That is why when I created Adam and Eve, I said, "It is very good." I am very pleased with all my creation, especially you, my precious child. When I see you, I see my Son, Jesus, in you. Live with this image in your heart.

My loving Father, thank you for creating me in your image and likeness. Thank you for giving me life. Thank you for loving me as your child.

RISE AND WALK

September 12

"Peter said, 'I have neither silver nor gold, but what I do have I give you: in the name of Jesus Christ the Nazarene, rise and walk.'" Acts 3:6

My child, I have given you the power to heal just like Peter and John and all my other disciples. Remember when I sent out 72 and they came back rejoicing? They were so happy when they could heal and cast out demons in my name. Yes, my name has power. Every time you call on me, I will be there for you. Your hands will become my hands; your words will become my words. My words have power to heal and to restore. It will be just like this crippled man who leaped up after Peter prayed in my name. His legs grew strong and he was able to follow Peter into the temple. This is my will. This is my desire that people become healed and able to enter into my temple to praise God. Go and do likewise.

Lord Jesus, I know you are our healer and our redeemer. Help me to have the courage to follow Peter's example and not be afraid to pray with others for healing.

GLORIOUS JOY

September 13

"Although you have not seen him you love him; even though you do not see him now yet believe in him, you rejoice with an indescribable and glorious joy, as you attain the goal of your faith, the salvation of your souls." 1 Peter 1: 8-9

In my vision I saw a royal wedding couple standing on the balcony of the palace waving in front of a huge crowd of people. They kissed and they smiled with total joy. Jesus said to me, "My loving child, this is the joy that you will experience when you enter into my kingdom. You will be welcomed into my wedding feast. A huge banquet will be prepared for you. I will be standing next to you on the balcony waving towards all the saints who have already reached their goal of salvation. Your heart will be overflowing with joy. Not because of all the people cheering for you, but because you have finally reached union with me. We became one. Our love for each other is like the bride and groom in your vision."

I love you, Lord, with my whole heart, mind, body and soul. You have filled me with so much love and joy. Praise you, Jesus.

PATHS OF LIFE

September 14

"You have made known to me the paths of life; you will fill me with joy in your presence." Acts 2:28

In my vision I saw myself walking behind Jesus who was clearing the path in front of me through a jungle. He told me to follow him closely and not to worry. As the path became more difficult and muddy, he carried me so that I would not sink into the mud. When the path led to a beautiful spot with flowers he told me to rest and to enjoy the scenery. At the end of the path, we arrived at the beach and I saw a beautiful blue sky and ocean like the ones I have seen in Hawaii. What joy! I knew I was in heaven. Jesus said to me, "My loving child, this vision showed you that as long as you are with me you have nothing to fear for I will protect you and guide you all the way through your entire life. As long as you stay close to me you will have no worries whatsoever. You will be filled with my love and joy."

What a beautiful vision! Lord Jesus, let me always remember that you are walking before me. I have nothing to fear.

WORK FOR FOOD

September 15

"Do not work for food that perishes but for the food that endures for eternal life, which the Son of Man will give you." John 6:27

My precious child, earthly food only nourishes your body. But within a few hours you will be hungry again. Spiritual food is my body and my blood. When you eat my body and drink my blood you will have eternal life and you will never hunger and thirst again. You will be filled with the Holy Spirit and you will feel satisfied. Your soul will be nourished and transformed into my likeness. You will be filled with my grace and power as St. Stephen was. Your face will glow with the light of Christ. You will have the zeal to proclaim my good news to others. You will be able to endure all pain and suffering for my sake. Work for food that does not perish and you will be satisfied.

To work for you, Lord, is my delight; for your work is easy and your yoke is light.

LIKE A SHEEP

September 16

"Like a sheep he was led to the slaughter, and as a lamb before its shearer is silent, so he opened not his mouth." Acts 8:32

In my vision I saw Jesus being nailed to the cross. He opened his mouth with pain, but no sound came out of it. Jesus said to me, "There is no greater love than one who lays down his life for another. I willingly died on the cross for you, my loving child. I want you to have eternal life with me in heaven. Love is sacrificing for another. A mother goes through hard labor with pain to give birth to her child. A father works day and night to provide for his family. True love is giving and sacrificing for the well being of another. There is no short cut. Love requires sacrifice. Like a sheep I willingly gave up my life for you on the cross. You are precious to me. I have redeemed you with my body and blood. Every time you eat my body and drink my blood you will realize how much I love you."

Lord Jesus, I am forever grateful for what you have done for me. Let me never be separated from you.

SCRIPTURES

September 17

"Then he opened their minds to understand the scriptures." Luke 24:45

My child, read the scriptures as my love letters to you. Every word in the scriptures has deep and profound meanings. They speak the truth. They reveal what is real in the spiritual world. Read them daily and they will open your eyes. The scriptures will enlighten you in all you do. They will open your heart and mind to see the reality according to God's point of view. They will show you solutions to your problems in new ways. They will open doors to areas of life where you are struggling and having trouble. They will bring blessings to you and your family. My words will set you free. They will transform you and change you into my image and likeness. You will be led through the scriptures into my kingdom. The scriptures are the way to my heart. Read them often. Ponder them in your heart.

Lord, I love to read the scripture. Your words are priceless. Thank you for giving me such a wonderful treasure.

SWORD

September 18

"Behold, this child is destined for the fall and rise of many in Israel and to be a sign that will be contradicted and you yourself a sword will pierce so that the thoughts of many hearts may be revealed." Luke 2:34-35

My precious child, bring all your sufferings to me and I will unite them together with my heart. It is only through suffering that you will grow. Your heart will be softened with compassion and mercy. Every suffering is precious. Embrace all your trials and you will grow stronger spiritually through your suffering. No pain, no gain. Through suffering you will know what others go through. You will understand their heart. You will be able to help them. Without suffering, there is no redemption or healing. So endure all. Surrender all. Only then will your heart be united with ours.

Loving Jesus, I give you my heart. Let me never to be separated from you.

GREAT LOVE

September 19

"So I tell you, her many sins have been forgiven; hence, she has shown great love." Luke 7:47

Love covers all sins. Do not focus on your own sinfulness but on how much I love you. My love heals all broken hearts. My love overcomes all sinfulness. It is like snow falling on a dirty street. The ground will be all cleaned by the melted snow. No more dirt, no more grime. All cleaned by the pure white snow. Love conquers all evil. Love can change a person from darkness into light. Love melts all hatred, resentment and anger. Love brings joy and healing. Love never fails. Love conquers all. Be my love to everyone you meet each day. Give my blessings to them. Shower them with my love. Let each day be a day of great love. Be my heart. Be my hands to hold and to embrace all those who need my love.

Yes, Lord, I will go and spread your love to all I meet today. You are all I need. Give me more of your healing love.

COMPANIONS OF JESUS

September 20

"Observing the boldness of Peter and John and perceiving them to be uneducated, ordinary men, the leaders, elders and scribes were amazed, and they recognized them as the companions of Jesus." Acts 4:13

Are you my companion? Do you enjoy sitting and talking with me? Are you lonely when you are away from me? Do you miss me? I would love to be your companion. Invite me into your daily life. I like to share my thoughts with you on everything. I like to go places with you and meet all your friends. I like sitting next to you while you are resting. I would love to eat with you and listen to all your joys and problems. Do you not realize that I long for you? Every morning you come to receive me in the Eucharist. But when you are outside the church it seems like you live your life without me. Can you see how much I enjoy your companionship? I love you more than you can ever imagine.

Lord Jesus, I am heartily sorry for not inviting you into every area of my life. Please be with my companion today and every day.

HUMBLE

September 21

"When dealing with the arrogant, he is stern, but to the humble he shows kindness." Proverbs 3:34

My precious child, humility means total dependence on me. An arrogant person thinks that he can do all things well by himself. But a humble person is one who knows his true ability. Without me you can do nothing. Everything you have is given by my Father. A truly humble person knows his own limitations and will not be proud of his own efforts. A humble person asks for my help before he starts any project. An arrogant person goes out alone and thinks that he can do it all by himself. A truly humble person is one who is understanding and kind. He is willing to listen and to admit when he is wrong. He is compassionate with others. He does not judge others harshly. Imitate me, my child, for I am humble and meek.

Lord, I am helpless without you. You are my life and my salvation. Help me to be humble and meek like you.

DRINKS MY BLOOD

September 22

"Amen, amen, I say to you, unless you eat the flesh of the Son of Man and drink his blood, you do not have life within you. Whoever eats my flesh and drinks my blood has eternal life, and I will raise him on the last day." John 6:53-54

My precious child, did you know that the Jews in the ancient times could not have any blood in their food? That was why they had to drain all the animals' blood before they could eat the food. They believed that blood was the essence of life. Whoever ate an animal with the blood in it would be contaminated. Everyone who drinks my blood will be transformed into my image and likeness and will have abundant life. My blood will give you new energy, strength and power to overcome all evil. My blood will cleanse all your sins and even the past sins committed by your ancestors. When you eat my body and drink my blood it is like receiving a blood transfusion. It will revitalize you and will bring you closer to me. You become my blood relative. You become my loving child.

Thank you, Lord, for giving us your body and blood every morning at Mass. It is always the highlight of my day.

RESTED

September 23

"And God rested on the seventh day from all his works." Hebrews 4:4

Rest in me, my child. Rest upon me as my disciple John did at the last supper. Listen to my heart beat. Stay close to me. Unless you rest you cannot work effectively for me. It is important that you get enough sleep every night and rest on Sundays. Your body needs it. Your soul needs it. You need to spend quiet time alone with me. Just sit by my feet and put your head on my lap. I will refresh you and renew you. I will restore you. You will be able to accomplish great things when you rest in me. Only then will you be doing my work and fulfilling all my desires. Only then will you be doing my will.

Thank you, Lord, for always being there for me, even in my sleep. I want to rest in your merciful and divine heart.

REJOICE

September 24

"Rejoice, O young man, when you are young and let your heart be glad in the days of your youth." Ecclesiastes 11:9

My child, do not worry about tomorrow. Enjoy each day as in your youth. Follow the ways of your heart and rejoice daily. Enjoy all the blessings that I have given you. Give thanks for everything that you have. Give praise to your loving Father who has provided you with all you need. Give thanks for our love for you. Let all your days be filled with the Holy Spirit, like the sun shining on a green pasture. Let your mouth sing songs of praise like the birds in the air. Let your lips be as sweet as honey and your heart as pure as gold. Let every part of your body praise God for we love you with an everlasting love. We will always be there for you. Rejoice and be glad!

O Lord, my heart sings with joy. You are an awesome God! I can never thank you enough for all you have done for me.

RIGHT AND JUST

September 25

"To do what is right and just is more acceptable to the Lord than sacrifice." Proverbs 21:3

My beloved, every action you do to please me is worth more than any sacrifice you can offer to atone for your sins. Your good deeds will benefit not only yourself, but everyone around you. You are actively building my kingdom with your kindness and mercy towards others. To those who love much, much is forgiven. Love brings joy to my heart. Love without action is like a noisy gong. Only doing what is right and just in my eyes is pleasing to me. When you obey my commandments and listen to my teachings, you are acting as my child and storing treasures in heaven. Nothing is wasted when you do what I have planned for you for each day. When you follow my instructions, every action will succeed. Do not waste your time regretting what you have failed to do but to start each day with a new page.

Loving Father, I only want to do what is right and just in your eyes. Give me the wisdom to follow your son Jesus in everything I do today.

THIS CHILD

September 26

"Whoever receives this child in my name receives me, and whoever receives me receives the one who sent me." Luke 9:48

Each child is unique. Each child needs someone to guide him and to help him. Whatever you do to the least, you do it to me. Receive them in your arms. Embrace them and love them. The way to show how much you love me is to love those who are most vulnerable and least lovable. Only through loving others will your heart expand. You will see the beauty in giving. You will be able to receive my love through them. The more you give, the more you will receive. It is a two-way street. Your life will be enriched when you help a child grow into my image and likeness. You will be rewarded a hundredfold. Give generously. Love deeply.

Lord, fill my heart with love and compassion for everyone. Open my eyes to enable me to see them as you see them.

MY SERVANT

September 27

"You are my servant, he said to me, Israel, through whom I show my glory." Isaiah 49:3

In my vision I saw myself as a servant wearing a little white apron and a white hat. I stood in front of my master, waiting for his order. Jesus said to me, "My precious child. To be a faithful servant you must first listen to what I say to you. Never do things on your own without first consulting me and then follow my instructions. It is important that you spend quiet time listening to me before you start any project or chores. Only then will you truly become my servant. Only then will you become an effective worker of mine. Without spending quality time alone with me first, you will be busy doing your own agenda and your own will. To be my faithful servant, you must carry out my mission to the end as did Mother Teresa and Pope John Paul II. It means long suffering and self sacrificing. Go and do likewise."

Here I am, Lord, I come to do your will. Please give me the strength to carry out all that you have planned for me to do till the end of my life.

CALL DOWN FIRE

September 28

"Lord, do you want us to call down fire from heaven to consume them?" Luke 9:54

My loving child, always conquer evil with love. Never an eye for an eye. Give more to those who hate you and persecute you. Only through love can you conquer the evil one. Only through sacrifice and suffering will you be able to change this world. Evil will only breed evil. Evil kills and destroys. Love blooms. Do not condemn others for you do not know their hearts. Some actions might not seem loving but their intention is pure. Some actions seem very honorable but their motive might be evil. So judge not and you will not be judged. Let no words of malice come out of your mouth, only words of encouragement and kindness. Your words have power. You can build or destroy a person. Use loving words to build my kingdom here on earth.

Loving Father, only you have the words of everlasting life. Help me to guard my mouth before I speak, that I might speak love and kindness to others, even to my enemies.

PROMISE

September 29

"When God made the promise to Abraham, since he had no one greater by whom to swear, he swore by himself, and said, 'I will indeed bless you and multiply you.'" Hebrews 6:13-14

How can I not bless you when every morning you receive the body of my son Jesus in the Eucharist? Your flesh is no longer yours, but belongs to Jesus. Your thoughts have been changed and conformed to my son's thoughts. You are my child. I love you as much as I love my son Jesus. The same words I spoke when Jesus was baptized in the river Jordan, I am speaking to you now, "You are my beloved in whom I am well pleased." Your children are my children. I love them even more than you love them. Your family is my family. I will bless each one of them with my infinite love. They will know me through you. Have faith in me and trust in me.

Loving Father, my God and my Lord, your love for me is more than I can imagine. I am so blessed to be your beloved child. I worship you and I adore you.

MY VINDICATOR

September 30

"But as for me, I know that my Vindicator lives, and that he will at last stand forth upon the dust." Job 19:25

My loving child, I am not your persecutor but your redeemer. I only want what is best for you. You can trust in me. I have already paid the price for your salvation. There is no need to fear. You are in my book of life. Your name is carved in the palms of my hands. I will never forget you or forsake you for you are mine. Let no one tell you otherwise. You are a child of God and we dwell in you. Your body is our holy temple. Take good care of yourself. I will always be at your side like a good lawyer who will make sure that you regain your freedom and get all that you deserve to have. I am your vindicator, your liberator and your helper. You can lean on me and trust that all will be well.

Lord Jesus, I thank you for redeeming me and saving me. I will trust you always. You are the savior of the world.

ANGELS IN HEAVEN

October 1

"See that you do not despise one of these little ones, for I say to you that their angels in heaven always look upon the face of my heavenly Father." Matthew 18:10

My precious child, your guardian angel is always with you. You are never alone. Every human being has a guardian angel, but not everyone listens or pays attention to his angel. Those who do are blessed. Angels are messengers from God and they only want what is best for you. Be attentive to their presence. Call on them when you are in need. When you pray, imagine your prayers being carried in a bowl by your angel directly to my heavenly Father. Every prayer is heard. Every petition is important to my Father. He is concerned about you as much as I am with you. Your angel will never leave you. They are always by your side. They watch over you day and night, because you are precious to us.

My guardian angel, my protector and my guide, I thank you for always being there for me. Please pray for me.

MUSTARD SEED

October 2

"If you have faith the size of a mustard seed, you would say to this mulberry tree, 'Be uprooted and planted in the sea,' and it would obey you." Luke 17:6

Faith is to believe in me. For me, nothing is impossible. Look at a tiny seed that I have created. It can bloom into a large tree bearing beautiful green leaves and juicy fruits. When you have faith in your heart, you also can do great things. It will be easy for you with my help. Everything you touch can be changed. Remember how the shadow of Peter healed a sick person who had faith in him. So it is with you, when you have total faith and trust in me. All power comes from me. Never be separated from me. Without me, you can do nothing. With me, we can change the world.

Lord, you are the miracle worker. You have the everlasting word. I believe in you and I trust in you.

MOVED WITH COMPASSION

October 3

"But a Samaritan traveler who came upon him was moved with compassion at the sight." Luke 10:33

My loving child, let your heart be open. Do not be afraid to suffer or to sacrifice for the love of others. It is only through love that you will have joy in life. It is not what you do for me or for others that matters but the condition of your heart. Without love, all is done in vain. With love, all acts of mercy and compassion are like pearls gathered into the treasure chest in heaven. Nothing is wasted. Mercy and compassion are what I want. Love and forgiveness are what matter. Many works are done out of pride. Only works done in the name of mercy and compassion are true love. Do every act with great love and compassion for others. There is no greater love than laying down one's life for others. Imitate me in all you do. Follow my example in your daily life. Love passionately. Love without ceasing.

Transform and change my heart, O Lord. Mold me into your likeness. Fill me with your love and compassion.

ANXIOUS AND WORRIED

October 4

"Martha, Martha, you are anxious and worried about many things. There is need of only one thing. Mary has chosen the better part and it will not be taken from her." Luke 10:41-42

When you focus your energy on worldly things you will feel anxious and worried. But when you focus your attention on me and on heavenly things you will experience peace. Everything in this world is passing while spiritual things are eternal. When you see the big picture with my eyes you will not be worried about anything for you will know that I am in control. With me at your side you have nothing to be anxious about. Even though everything might seem chaotic with me there is peace. I care about every detail in your day. I know every hair on your head. There is nothing that happens in your life that I do not know about. So focus your day with me by your side.

Lord, I want to sit at your feet as Mary did and listen to your words of wisdom. Fill me with your peace.

FRIEND

October 5

"Friend, lend me three loaves of bread, for a friend of mine has arrived at my house from a journey and I have nothing to offer him." Luke 11:5-6

In my vision I saw a big brother holding his little sister's hand walking down the street. Jesus said to me, "My precious child and my good friend. I am your big brother who loves you more than you can ever imagine. I am always ready to protect you and to guide you. Give me your hand and I will lead you. I will help you every step of the way. You can count on my being there for you always. I will hold you up when you are tired and weary. I will help you to climb the steep hills. I will carry you when you can no longer walk. You are my friend and my treasure. I will never leave you. I will always be at your side. I will comfort you when you are sad and rejoice with you when you are happy. I will give you rest when you are weary. Lean on me."

What a good friend I have in you, Jesus! You are more precious than jewel. I thank you for being my friend.

CURSE

October 6

"Christ ransomed us from the curse of the law by becoming a curse for us, for it is written, 'Cursed be anyone who hangs on a tree', that the blessings of Abraham might be extended to the Gentiles through Christ Jesus, so that we might receive the promise of the spirit through faith." Galatians 3:13-14

In my vision I saw a balancing scale for measuring things. On one side it had all the blessings and on the other side it had all the curses. When the blessings were abundant, the curses fell off the scale. Jesus said to me, "You have all my blessings, my child. There is no room for any curses in your life, because you are mine. Only blessings will follow you all the days of your life. Be a blessing to others. Help them to get rid of any curses that may have been put upon them. You have the power and the ability to remove all curses in my name. Use the authority that I have given to all my children. Pour your blessings upon everyone. I am with you."

Thank you, Lord, for dying on the cross for me and for setting me free from all the curses. I feel so blessed.

BAPTIZED INTO CHRIST

October 7

"For all of you who were baptized into Christ have clothed yourselves with Christ." Galatians 3:27

My child, the minute you were baptized into Christ all your sins were washed clean. Then the Holy Spirit descended upon you. From that day on, you became our child. My Father in heaven is very pleased with you. You started to act like me and talk like me. Your mouth will speak the truth. Your heart will love like mine with mercy and compassion. See how much you look like your brothers and sisters? See how you all laugh alike? See how you speak with a similar accent? This is what happened when you were baptized into Christ. You are transformed into my image and likeness. Your thoughts are like my thoughts. Your heart rejoices like mine.

Lord Jesus, I want to be like you more and more each day. Change me and mold me.

GIVE THANKS

October 8

"Ten were cleansed, were they not? Where are the other nine? Has none but this foreigner returned to give thanks to God?" Luke 17:17-18

All ten lepers were healed. But only one was saved because this person realized who I am. He believed in me and he was thankful for what I had done for him. His faith in me saved him. Anyone who believes in me and calls me Lord is saved. A grateful heart leads to conversion. Give thanks for everything that I have done for you. A grateful heart is a loving heart. A grateful heart is a joyful heart. My child, live each day with a grateful and joyful heart. You are special to me. I will always provide all your needs. Be like this foreigner; have total trust in me. All you need to do is to ask and I will grant your heart's desires. My compassionate heart hears all your prayers and petitions. Ask and give thanks.

You are my almighty God! I love you Lord with all my heart. I thank you and praise you all the days of my life.

GIVE ALMS

October 9

"But as to what is within, give alms, and behold, everything will be clean for you." Luke 11:41

My loving child, when you give alms you are mindful of other people's needs. You will have more love and understanding in your heart. Your heart will be moved with justice and compassion. When you give alms your generosity will wash away all your sins. You will reap what you have sown. Your heart will be softened. Instead of judging, your heart will be moved with pity. A generous heart is a loving heart. Your sins are forgiven because you have loved much. Whatever you do to the least you do it to me. And I will never cease to repay you for every good deed you have done to all those I love. You will be blessed abundantly. Your children and children's children will be blessed also. It is like a domino effect. What goes around will affect you deeply. Give generously to all who ask from you.

Lord, give me a generous heart so that I will be as loving as you are to all those in need. Help me to give alms to everyone who asks from me.

FRUIT

October 10

"The fruit of the Spirit is love, joy, peace, patience, kindness, generosity, faithfulness, gentleness, self-control." Galatians 5:22-23

In my vision I saw a large tree with different fruits hanging from its branches. Jesus said to me, "You must first desire the fruit. Then you need to pick it off the tree and eat it. By consuming the fruit it becomes part of you. All fruits on this tree are for you, my child. They are for all those who desire them. The fruits will only grow if the soil is right and when it is watered often. Pray and ask for the Holy Spirit often. Invoke the name of the Holy Spirit every time you pray especially before you start any project or go someplace. Invite him into your heart. Listen to his promptings and your reward will be great. You will be filled with his light and his healing power. Be fruitful."

Come, Holy Spirit, come. You are my comforter and my guiding light. Fill me with your love, joy and peace.

BLOOD OF CHRIST

October 11

"For if the blood of goats and bulls and the sprinkling of a heifer's ashes can sanctify those who are defiled so that their flesh is cleansed, how much more will the blood of Christ, who through the eternal spirit offered himself unblemished to God, cleanse our conscience from dead works to worship the living God." Hebrews 9:13-14

In my vision I saw Jesus seems to be braiding a red and a white yarn together. Then I saw my blood being mingled with his blood and bound together with his living water. Jesus said to me, "I am a God of justice and of love. For every sin you have committed there are consequences. The wage of sin is death. That is why I had to shed my blood and die on the cross for you. I paid your ransom. You are mine. I covered you with my precious blood. I saved you from eternal damnation. I redeemed you from the evil one. You are now clothed in Christ with my light. You are no longer a slave to sin but a precious child close to my heart. You have been washed clean with my blood. Go and sin no more.

Lamb of God, you who take away the sins of the world have mercy on me. Jesus, you are truly my savior and my redeemer.

BE UNITED

October 12

"I urge you, brothers, in the name of our Lord Jesus Christ, that all of you agree with what you say, and that there be no divisions among you, but that you be united in the same mind and in the same purpose." 1 Corinthians 1:10

In my vision I saw the universe moving in unison. The small planets surround the big suns. Each sun was moving according to God's plan. God said to me, "So it is with my kingdom. Each church is like the sun. It is surrounded by all the ministers in the church. Everyone is revolving around the church. All are doing good deeds for building up my kingdom. Everyone is needed to make this universe a better place in which to live. Everyone is called according to my plan. There should be no jealousy and division, for you have one God and one Lord. Everyone who does my will is a member of my family."

Lord God, you are the creator of this beautiful universe. I worship you and I adore you.

CHILDREN OF LIGHT

October 13

"Live as children of light, for light produces every kind of goodness and righteousness and truth." Ephesians 5:8-9

In my vision I saw Jesus standing in the middle. All his children were standing in a circle facing him in the center. Their faces were all aglow with his light. Their backs were in the dark. When one of them turned away from Jesus, his face became dark and he walked away from the light. Jesus said to me, "Stay close to me, my precious child. Always be focused on me. Do not turn your back against me. For without my light you will walk in darkness. You will fall and stumble. When you find yourself lost just search for the light. I will always be there to guide you. Seek my face and you will see the light. Follow the light and you will find me. I am in the center of your life. I will never leave you or forsake you."

Jesus, you are the light of the world. You are my light and my salvation. Without your light, there is no hope.

PHARISEE

October 14

"The Pharisee took up his position and spoke this prayer to himself, 'O God, I thank you that I am not like the rest of humanity – greedy, dishonest, adulterous – or even like this tax collector." Luke 18:11

My child, notice how the Pharisee prayed to himself. He was not there to praise me or to thank me. It was all about himself and how good he was. He felt so righteous and so perfect in his own eyes. He considered himself better than others, especially better than the tax collector who was raising his eyes to heaven and asking God's forgiveness. It breaks my heart to know that there are many people who pray just as this Pharisee did. My loving child, never look down on others. My heart goes out to the lowly and the humble. They will be filled with my grace and power. They are the ones I choose to be my disciples. Imitate them. Confess your sins and be humble yourself. And I will fill you with the Holy Spirit.

My sweet Jesus, I am heartily sorry for all my sins. I have been proud so many times like this Pharisee. I have compared myself with others. Please forgive me. With your help, I hope to never sin against you who deserve all my love.

THE FIRST

October 15

"The first is this: Hear, O Israel! The Lord our God is Lord alone! You shall love the Lord your God with all your heart, with all your soul, with all your mind and with all your strength. The second is this: You shall love your neighbor as yourself." Mark 12:29-30

In my vision I saw a large wooden cross. Jesus said to me, "My precious child, this wooden cross is a perfect example for you to learn how to live each day. The vertical beam is your love for God and the horizontal beam is your arm reaching out to all your neighbors. Without the vertical beam, the horizontal beam will fall. First, you must be filled with my love and strength before you can love others. Without me you will not be able to reach out to the unlovable and the least of society. They would become a burden too heavy for you to carry. But when your love is grounded in me, like the vertical beam of the cross, you will be able to carry your cross as I did on Good Friday. Remain in my love and I in you."

Lord Jesus, thank you for dying on the cross for me. You are my savior and my redeemer. Teach me to reach out to others.

GREAT NATION

October 16

"For what great nation is there that has gods so close to it as the Lord, our God, is to us whenever we call upon him?" Deuteronomy 4:7

My precious child, see how a bee colony all works together in harmony and serves their queen bee? Every bee has a job and is important in building their honeycomb. So it is with a great nation that serves me. I am always ready to help you when you pray to me. Any nation that follows all my commandments will prosper for my laws are for the good of all those who serve me. Without my commandments there is no harmony or peace, only chaos and destruction. Pray for your nation, my child. It is slowly turning away from me as the people in the Old Testament did. Everyone was doing what they pleased. Without me there is no salvation. Pray that this nation will repent and come back to me.

O Jesus, please show us the way to go back to our Father in heaven. Bless this nation and protect us from all harm.

NEVER THIRST

October 17

"Everyone who drinks this water will be thirsty again; but whoever drinks the water I shall give will never thirst; the water I shall give will become in him a spring of water welling up to eternal life." John 4:13-14

In my vision I saw a stream of running water coming down from a snow-capped mountain. The water was so clear that you could see every pebble and rock beneath the water. Any dirt or mud was washed clean by this running water. It flowed and flowed without ceasing. There were little fishes and small animals around this fresh water. Jesus said to me, "My word is like this spring of water. It is always moving. It can mold and change people's hearts. It removes all your guilt and shame from the past. It heals all your hurts and wounds. It refreshes your soul and strengthens your body. It gives you hope and joy. Come to my living water daily and drink deeply. I will comfort you and wash you clean."

Lord, pour your living water into my heart. Cleanse me of all my sins. Jesus, I thirst for you.

ACKNOWLEDGES ME

October 18

"Everyone who acknowledges me before others, the Son of Man will acknowledge before the angels of God." Luke 12:8

My child, if you were my best friend would I not introduce you to all my friends and family? So it is with us. If I am your best friend would you introduce me to all your friends and family? I knock at the door of your heart. I long to be a part of your family. I want to join your circle of friends and be recognized as your best friend. When you talk with your friends do you often talk about your loved ones? Am I one of your loved ones? Am I worthy of your praises? Thank you for each time that you have acknowledged me in front of others. Never cease to talk about me to others, my friend.

You are my best friend, Lord Jesus. You are worthy of all my praises. Thank you for being my friend. I will always treasure you and acknowledge you in front of others.

VIRTUE

October 19

"None of the crimes he committed shall be remembered against him; he shall live because of the virtue he has practiced." Ezekiel 18:22

In my vision I saw a beautiful white garment. Jesus said to me, "You see this white garment and how beautiful it is? The virtues are like this white garment. They are pleasing to God. When you live a virtuous life, all you do will be pleasing to my Father in heaven. However, when one is filled with sin the white garment will eventually become like a rag. It will only be fit to be thrown out. My dear child, keep yourself from any wrongdoing day in and day out. Go to God for reconciliation often. I am always ready to forgive you and to wash you clean. Keep your white garment spotless. Practice your virtues of faith, hope and charity daily. Above all, love your neighbor as I have loved you. Go in peace."

My loving Father, thank you for this vision. With your help, I hope to keep myself spotless. Help me to overcome all my sinful ways.

VIGILANT

October 20

"Blessed are those servants whom the master finds vigilant on his arrival." Luke 12:37

My precious child, I long to be with you for eternity. I have already prepared a place for you in heaven. Be patient and be watchful. I will come when you are least expecting me. Live each day as your last day here on earth. It is not how many chores you are doing, but how many souls that you have loved that matters. It is the quality time that you spend alone with me and all my loved ones that counts. It is sitting by my feet and listening to me. It is doing the will of my Father. Do not worry or have any anxieties whatsoever. I come not to condemn but to save. I come to welcome you into my Father's house. I have prepared a banquet for you to celebrate with all your loved ones. I will come soon.

Jesus, I can hardly wait for that day when I will see you face to face and to enjoy the banquet with you in heaven. Jesus, I trust in you.

ON FIRE

October 21

"I have come to set the earth on fire, and how I wish it were already blazing!" Luke 12:49

My child, everyone who asks for the Holy Spirit will be rewarded. You have prepared your heart to receive the Holy Spirit. It is my desire that everyone be filled with the Holy Spirit. But many people do not believe in me or love me. Their hearts are closed. I cannot open them unless they invite me in. I stand at the door of their hearts and knock. I long to give each one my Spirit. Go and pray with all those who are ready to receive. The Holy Spirit will teach you what to do and say. He will give you all the gifts you need to be my disciple. Do not be afraid to step out. Be on fire for me.

Come Holy Spirit! Come and set our hearts on fire for Jesus. Come and renew the face of the earth.

YOU WILL PERISH

October 22

"If you do not repent, you will all perish as they did." Luke 13:5

In my vision I saw a house infested with termites. Jesus said to me, "A person with sin is like a house full of termites. At the beginning there are only a few small termites. Almost unnoticeable. But if they are not exterminated and removed they will gradually spread to the entire house. Pretty soon the wood will be full of holes and begin to crumble. So it is with sin. Sin always starts small. Eventually it will affect every part of you. It grows and grows. Unless you repent, it can destroy you. The earlier you confess your sins, the easier to get rid of them. The longer you hold onto your sins, the harder it is to remove them from your soul. When you go to reconciliation I will pour my precious blood and graces over you. You will be as white as snow again."

Thank you, Lord, for this revelation. Now I can see how important it is that I go to confession as often as possible. You always welcome me with your open arms.

GOD OF JUSTICE

October 23

"The Lord is a God of justice, who knows no favorites. Though not unduly partial towards the weak, yet he hears the cry of the oppressed." Sirach 35: 12-13

My precious child, I am a God of justice, but I am also a God of compassion and mercy. All those who are hungry and poor, their prayers will always be heard. My heart goes out to all those who are underprivileged and suffering. For I was treated unjustly while I was the son of a carpenter. People looked down on me and despised me. They had no mercy towards me while they crucified me on the cross. I asked for prayers, but my disciples all fell asleep in the garden of Gethsemane. I can relate to all those who are oppressed and helpless. I hear their cry. Do not be afraid to intercede for all those who are suffering. I will answer your prayers.

My God and my Lord, you have a heart of compassion for the poor. You always answer my prayers. I praise you and I thank you.

YEAST

October 24

"To what shall I compare the kingdom of God? It is like yeast that a woman took and mixed in with three measures of wheat flour until the whole batch of dough was leavened." Luke 13:20-21

The yeast is like your faith, my child. It needs to be worked on. It needs to be incorporated into your daily life. It needs to be nourished with prayer, communion and spiritual readings. It takes time to see the result. It takes effort and energy to strengthen your faith. Even though it started very small it will grow and affect everyone around you. You are my yeast which I can use to leaven others. It is not your own effort but mine that leavens the entire batch. All you do is surrender and be willing to be kneaded and molded by me. Your joy and reward will be great.

I am all yours, my Lord. Knead me and mold me into your image and likeness. I am here to do your will.

EVILDOERS

October 25

"I do not know where you are from. Depart from me, all you evildoers!" Luke 13:27

Who are the evildoers? They are those who are selfish and self-centered and do not follow the commandments of my Father. They do everything according to their own hearts and desires. They are not obedient to the will of my Father. They think they do not need God in their lives. They do not have the right conscience. In their minds there is no right and wrong. But you, my child, are obedient and pleasing to me. Your desire is to be close to me and to serve me. For you, life on this earth is to do my Father's will. Come, my faithful servant. Come and I will nourish you with my body and blood, for you are my loving child. I love you deeply.

Lord Jesus, I consecrate my life to you and to our Father in heaven. You are the center of my life. I want only to serve you.

DWELLING PLACE

October 26

"Through him the whole structure is held together and grows into a temple sacred in the Lord; in him you also are being built together into a dwelling place of God in the Spirit." Ephesians 2:21-22

In my vision I saw a little house built with the Eucharistic hosts instead of bricks and mortar. There was smoke coming out of the chimney. Jesus said to me, "My precious child, each time you receive my body and drink my blood you are building my dwelling place within your heart. A house must be kept clean. Do you not clean your home at least once a month? It is the same with your soul. It is important to go to reconciliation often, at least once a month. No matter how hard you try to be sinless, there is always dust and dirt. The smoke in your vision is the Holy Spirit. Keep the fire going by invoking the Holy Spirit often. This way you will be filled with his gifts of loving and caring. The Holy Spirit who dwells in your heart will be your love for all who need me."

Wow! What an awesome vision. Thank you, Jesus. I invite you to dwell in my heart. Fill me with your Holy Spirit.

MY PRAYER

October 27

"This is my prayer: that your love may increase ever more and more in knowledge and every kind of perception, to discern what is of value, so that you may be pure and blameless for the day of Christ, filled with the fruit of righteousness that comes through Jesus Christ for the glory and praise of God." Philippians 1:9-11

When you pray, my child, focus your attention on me. Do not babble with too many words, but pray from your heart with words that cry out from the depth of your soul. I know all your needs and petitions before you ask. What I long to hear is your love and gratitude for me. May your prayers be filled with praise and thanksgiving. Prayer is not always talking. It is like two lovers who can just sit next to each other and hold hands without saying a word. And yet, their hearts are content and are filled with love for each other. That is what I long for from you. Come and sit next to me and listen to me.

Jesus, my love and my King. My heart longs to be with you. Pour more of your love into my heart. I adore you, my Jesus.

EXALTS HIMSELF

October 28

"For everyone who exalts himself will be humbled, but the one who humbles himself will be exalted." Luke 14:11

In my vision I saw two persons sitting on a seesaw going up and down. Jesus said to me, "My child, the vision you just saw revealed to you that when you sit at the lower end of the seesaw you will surely to be lifted up. It is always wise to be humble, for in humility you will be exalted. You will be praised by all. But when you are proud, people around you will be jealous of you and they will make sure that you fall and tumble. Everything you have is from my Father. All the good you do is because of my grace. So there is nothing you can be proud of except to thank and praise my Father. He is the giver of all good. Be humble as I am humble."

Heavenly Father, I thank you for your love and grace. I praise you for I am wonderfully made. Everything I have is from you, Lord.

SALVATION

October 29

"Today salvation has come to this house because this man too is a descendant of Abraham. For the Son of Man has come to seek and to save what was lost." Luke 19:9-10

Salvation is for everyone, my child. But first, you must come and seek me like Zacchaeus. Even though he was a rich man, dressed in all his finery, he did not mind ruining his expensive clothes and making a fool of himself by climbing up a tree in order to see me. I will always come into your heart when you seek me. I will always bring salvation to you and your household when you invite me into your heart. For you, I have willingly suffered and died on the cross. Be transformed. Repent and change your ways like Zacchaeus. Your life will never be the same when you invite me into your abode.

Come, Lord Jesus, come! I welcome you with my whole heart. Come and live and dine with me. I invite you into my soul.

WORTHY TO SUFFER

October 30

"So they left the presence of the Sanhedrin, rejoicing that they had been found worthy to suffer dishonor for the sake of the name." Acts 5:41

My loving child, the greater your love for me the more you will be willing to suffer for my sake. How often has a parent said, "I wish I could be sick instead of my child." It pains parents to see their child with so much suffering when he is dying of cancer or any other serious disease. After Pentecost, my disciples were filled with the Holy Spirit. One of the fruits of the Holy Spirit is love. Their love for me was so great that they were willing to die as martyrs in my name. So ask my Father to fill you with the Holy Spirit. Ask him to fill you up with all the gifts and fruits of the Holy Spirit, especially with more love for me. Only then will you be rejoicing when you suffer for my sake. Ask and you shall receive."

Holy Spirit, I invite you to fill me with all your gifts and fruits so that I may love God more and more each day. Come, Holy Spirit, come!

LEAD THE BLIND

October 31

"I will lead the blind on their journey; by paths unknown I will guide them. I will turn darkness into light before them, and make crooked ways straight." Isaiah 42:16

In my vision I saw myself as a blind person placing my hand upon Jesus' shoulder as he led me into the unknown. As we walked he was telling me about the condition of the path, whether there were rocks or steps. Jesus said to me, "My precious child, let me always walk before you. This way I will protect you from all harm. Place your trust in me for I will never lead you astray. I will guide you and bring you to the right path. You will never be lost with me at your side. Hold onto me and never be separated from me. Do not get distracted from me. Focus on me and follow my directions. I will never forsake you. I will bring you into the light and the truth."

Lord, hold me tight. Never let me be separated from you. You are my guide and my protector.

POOR IN SPIRIT

November 1

"Blessed are the poor in spirit, for theirs is the kingdom of heaven." Matthew 5:3

In my vision I saw myself as an empty jar. Because I was empty, God was able to pour his grace and mercy into the jar. Jesus said to me, "My precious child, no one can come into the kingdom of heaven alone. Only those who are with me will be able to enter my kingdom. Those who are against me will never be able to enter into heaven, for heaven is where I am. Everyone who loves me and keeps my commandments will be able to enter my kingdom and enjoy eternal life with me. It is only with my grace and mercy that you are purified and sanctified. Those who are proud and think that they can earn heaven by their own merit will be disappointed. They are like the foolish bridesmaids who forgot the oil for their lanterns. The oil is my grace and mercy. Be humble and be hungry for my love."

Lord, without you I am nothing. I look forward to the day when I can join you in your kingdom of heaven. Thank you for your merciful love for me.

ALL ARE ALIVE

November 2

"He is not God of the dead, but of the living, for to him all are alive." Luke 20:38

My child, when I created Adam and Eve I had in mind that each human being would live with me for eternity. But when sin came into the Garden of Eden, everything changed. All those who love me and obey my laws will enjoy eternal life with me. But those who refuse to obey me and love me will be suffering hell. It is not my wish to send anyone there. But those who have so much hatred in their heart refuse to choose me. Every soul I have created is alive, for I am a God of the living. See how happy you were on the day when your children are born. They are your pride and joy. So it is with every soul I have created. Everyone is precious to me.

God of our universe, I love you and I worship you. You are my creator and my redeemer.

ABOUT THE PARABLES

November 3

"And when he was alone, those present along with the Twelve questioned him about the parables." Mark 4:10

In my vision I saw Jesus teaching a little child about something through a story. Jesus said to me, "A story or a parable is easier for a child to understand and to learn from about the truth. So it is with people who have little faith. They look but do not perceive. They hear but do not understand. But you are a child of God. You see with your spiritual eyes. You listen to my voice and you understand me. But those who do not know me do not understand the truth. That is why it is so important to be friends first before you try to teach anyone about me. Only then will they be open to receive the truth. Only then might they see the light. Only then might they grow to love me. Never stop sowing. Your job is to sow and leave the rest to me. Be faithful and be joyful!"

Jesus, please give me the seeds to sow everywhere I go. I am here to do your will wherever you want to send me.

ROUSE ONE ANOTHER

November 4

"We must consider how to rouse one another to love and good works." Hebrews 10:24

In my vision I saw a stone being thrown into a pond. The water immediately started to move in ripples. Jesus said to me, "Be my little rock that moves the water. Be the starter of motion for me. People are so comfortable in this world that they are not moving. They are asleep. They do not realize that the time to love and to do good works is running short. Every minute it is closer to judgment day. Do not waste any day without encouraging others to love me more. Barnabas, my disciple, encouraged Paul who became one of my most faithful apostles. Do the same for me, my child. Are you awake, my love?"

Lord, thank you for giving me another day to love and to serve you. Bless every work I do for your honor and glory.

EARTHLY THINGS

November 5

"Their minds are occupied with earthly things." Philippians 3:19

My precious child, everyone has only one mind. Your mind can be occupied with heavenly things or with earthly things. One cannot serve two masters at the same time. Let your mind be focused on building my kingdom here on earth. This way you will have treasures in heaven where you will be spending eternity with us. Let your mind be focused on holy and beautiful things from above. Sing songs of praise with thanksgiving in your heart. This way everyone who sees you will see me in you. Do not be concerned about what to eat or what to wear. All these will pass away. But my words will never pass away.

Lord Jesus, you have the words of everlasting life. I want to live each day with your peace, love and joy in my heart.

STRENGTH FOR EVERYTHING

November 6

"I have the strength for everything through him who empowers me." Philippians 4:13

In my vision I saw a person lifting weights and exercising. Jesus said to me, "My child, if you want to have strength, you need to build up your muscles. Prayer and fasting will give you the strength to do everything for me. It is through prayer that you will know how much I love you. I am with you in all you do. You are never alone. You do not carry the burden alone. You are yoked with me. The burden is on both of our shoulders. You can rely on me and trust in me that you are always under my protection and guidance. Fasting will foster humility and compassion, which are two qualities that are very pleasing to my Father. He will give you the strength you need."

Thank you, Lord, for this vision. A picture is a thousand words. Thank you for giving me the strength to do your will.

ENDURANCE

November 7

"You need endurance to do the will of God and receive what he has promised." Hebrews 10:36

In my vision I saw Jesus fell down three times. Jesus said to me, "My child, see how I carried my cross and fell down not once but three times. Even though every bone ached and I had nothing to eat or drink since the last supper I had to force myself to get up each time and to go on to Calvary. I knew that I had to be crucified and die on the cross for all the sins of the world. Without endurance my life on earth would have been wasted. All would have been in vain. So it is with you, my child. You need endurance to live each day with love in order to do good works. Without endurance you can never be my disciple. You will not reach the goal that I have planned for you. You will not be able to make a difference in this world. See how my disciples lived and worked until the day they died. They did not give up even when they were in great pain. Do likewise."

Lord Jesus, give me the courage and the endurance to carry my cross to the end of my life. Help me to get up each time I fall.

SEVEN TIMES

November 8

"If he wrongs you seven times in one day and returns to you seven times saying 'I am sorry,' you should forgive him." Luke 17:4

My precious child, unforgiveness is like a rock that a person is holding tightly in his hand. When that happens, his hand is clenched and cannot be opened to give or to receive love. Another version of unforgiveness is like a bottle stuck with a stopper. No grace can be poured into the bottle, which is the heart. Be forgiving always. Even seven times a day. Let your heart be set free from any anger, resentment and hurt. Hold no grudges against anyone. Only then will you be able to love freely and to enjoy life to the fullest. Only then will you be able to be free from any sadness and depression. With my grace and love in your heart, you will feel so joyful and so blessed.

Yes, Lord, I want to forgive everyone who has hurt me in the past. Please forgive me for all the times that I have sinned against you and others.

TEMPLE OF GOD

November 9

"Do you not know that you are the temple of God, and that the spirit of God dwells in you?" 1 Corinthians 3:16

It is my desire that you invite me into your heart, my loving child. I love to share my life with you. When I live in your heart your body will become my temple. So invite me in. Do not lock me out of your heart. Do not block my saving grace which I long to give to you. When you have me, you have everything. Imagine if a king or an emperor were coming to visit you. The first thing you would do is clean your house and put everything in order for his visit. You would cancel all your normal activities so that you could spend more time with him. So it is when you invite me into your heart. Your life will be transformed.

My heart longs for you, my King and my Lord. Please come and stay with me. I welcome you with my open arms.

KINGDOM OF GOD

November 10

"For behold, the kingdom of God is among you." Luke 17:21

In my vision I saw a map of the world. All the people in the world who have Christ in their hearts were lit up like Christmas trees. Jesus said to me, "It is my desire that everyone in this world be filled with my light. My kingdom will come and my will be done on earth only with your help. Everyone who is willing to be my disciple will help others to come to my light. Those in darkness, who are without light, need your help to lead them to the source of light. I am the light of the world. Anyone who believes in me will have the light of life. Oh how I long to see the entire world aglow with my light! My dear child, continue to build my kingdom here on earth. I will help you and will provide all you need."

Jesus, you are my light and my salvation. Only with your help can we change this world together.

DECEIVERS

November 11

"Many deceivers have gone out into the world, those who do not acknowledge Jesus Christ as coming in the flesh; such is the deceitful one and the antichrist." 2 John 1:7

My child, those who do not acknowledge me are deceivers for they bring glory only to themselves. But everyone who acknowledges me is a true believer. Whatever true believers do brings glory and honor to me and to my Father. Be ready always to acknowledge me in front of others. Tell them about all the miracles and healings that I have done. Be a witness for me. Only then can you become my true disciple. Do not follow anyone whose preaching is not about me, for they are on the wrong path. Go through the narrow gate where I await you. Follow no other.

Lord Jesus, I want to be a witness for you. I will acknowledge you and bring you glory and honor.

JUSTICE

November 12

"I tell you, he will see to it that justice is done for them speedily. But when the Son of Man comes, will he find faith on earth?" Luke 18:8

Justice is to give back what belongs to the other person. My child, everyone is created equal. Each human being is precious to me. When a poor person cries out to me, I will always answer his prayer. I am a God of justice. If everyone shared what he has with those less fortunate than himself there would be no one going hungry or without a home in this world. Many people are greedy and take more than their share. They have no love for others except themselves. They have no fear of the last judgment. But you, my precious child, you know better. Be generous to all who ask from you. Be my light and my hope to others.

Heavenly Father, you are a just God and you hear the cry of the poor. Help me to be a more charitable and generous person.

MESSENGER

November 13

"Behold, I am sending my messenger ahead of you, he will prepare your way before you." Luke 7:27

In my vision I saw a newspaper boy throwing newspaper in front of each house. God said to me, "My child, if you want to be my messenger, you need to get my word out to every person you meet. It is not your responsibility to know if people will read the newspaper or not. Your job is just to spread the good news so that those who are ready will be able to receive them. You are called to be my messenger. You are my hands and feet. I have chosen you. Will you go and carry out this important task that I have given you to do? Will you speak my words of love and encouragement to others for me? Will you comfort my people with tenderness and mercy? If you do, you are just as important to me as John the Baptist. Will you go for me?"

Yes, Lord, I will go as your messenger. I will go wherever you send me. Help me to have courage to proclaim your good news to everyone today.

ABOUND IN LOVE

November 14

"May the Lord make you increase and abound in love for one another and for all, just as we have for you." 1 Thessalonians 3:12

In my vision I saw Jesus with his heart exposed. It grew and grew as I was watching it. Jesus said to me, "My loving child, imitate me. Have you noticed that in a crowded place I always see the one who needs my love and attention the most? Like the time when I saw a man with a paralyzed hand. I healed him even on the Sabbath. Do likewise. Have more compassion for anyone who is less fortunate than you. They are hungry and thirsty for love. Give generously to all who ask from you. The more love you give away, the more you will receive back. I have loved you from the instant you were formed in your mother's womb. You are precious in my sight. Go and love others as I have loved you. May your heart be enlarged as in your vision. Ask the Holy Spirit to fill you with more love."

Lord Jesus, please fill me with the Holy Spirit. Enlarge my heart so that I will be able to love others as you have loved me.

HAVE SIGHT

November 15

"Jesus told him, 'Have sight; your faith has saved you.' He immediately received his sight and followed him, giving glory to God." Luke 18:42-43

My child, the way to see God is to pray unceasingly. The blind man was immobile, sitting on the ground begging. When I passed by him he did not stop crying out to me. Even though my disciples were trying to silence him he did not give up. Do the same, my child. Ask and you shall receive. Do not be afraid that you might look foolish to others. It is your faith that will save you. Continue to pray and pray. You know that I only want what is best for you. I will answer all your prayers. Be insistent and I will lead you to my Father in heaven. Come and have faith in me.

Thank you, Jesus, for the words of encouragement. I will pray and know that you will always answer my prayers. I have faith in you, Lord.

VISITATION

November 16

"They will smash you to the ground and your children within you, and they will not leave one stone upon another within you because you did not recognize the time of your visitation." Luke 19: 44

My loving child, my heart is breaking with sorrow because so few people recognize me when I am amongst them. They are so preoccupied with the world that they miss my visitation. Help them to know me and to see me in every aspect of their lives. The day will come when they will wish to have faith in me as you do. Only with me will they be able to go through all the trials and tribulations that they will face each day. Pray for them constantly. My heart aches for them to the point of weeping.

Lord Jesus, I want to console your broken heart. I will go and bring others closer to you. I will tell them how much they need you in their daily lives.

HOUSE ON ROCK

November 17

"Everyone who listens to these words of mine and acts on them will be like a wise man who built his house on rock." Matthew 7:24

In my vision I saw a lighthouse on the rocks at a harbor. There was a small house right behind the lighthouse. This lighthouse not only protected the house from the wind and the storm but also guided all the ships to safe harbor. Jesus said to me, "My precious child, I am the light of the world. I will protect you from all harm. If you stand behind me you will be safe. I will always be there for you. Stand firm. Stand on my words. My words are as solid as the rocks in your vision. They will help you through all your trials and difficulties. You will be guided by my light and protected from all the storms in your life. Stay close to me, my love."

Lord, let me never be separated from you. Your words are what I live on. Help me to build my house on your rock.

TWO BLIND MEN

November 18

"As Jesus passed on from there, two blind men followed him, crying out, 'Son of David, have pity on us!'" Matthew 9:27

My loving child, do you want to see? Many people are like these two blind men who spend their life without seeing. Do you know that every soul has spiritual eyes? Your spiritual eyes are just beginning to be opened. Pray to the Holy Spirit so that you will truly be able to see the world as I see it. You will see angels and demons. They are real. They are here in this world, but it takes spiritual eyes to see them. With your spiritual eyes you will also be able to see me and my Father, especially when you are praying. During prayer, your eyes will be opened. Ask my Father to open your eyes.

Loving Father, open my eyes, Lord. I want to see you. Son of David, have mercy on me. Come, Holy Spirit, fill me with your love.

SMALL SCROLL

November 19

"I took the small scroll from the angel's hand and swallowed it. In my mouth it was like sweet honey, but when I had eaten it, my stomach turned sour." Revelation 10:10

My words are like the orange juice that you drink every morning. It tastes really good in your mouth when you first swallow it. But when you drink it on an empty stomach it will turn sour. Read my words and study them with prayer and meditation. Chew on my words. Ponder and reflect on my words as my mother Mary did. Let my words reside in your heart and soul. Let them take effect on you. Let them direct your every action. My words are sweeter than honey and they will comfort you and console you.

Thank you, Jesus, for your words of wisdom. I will always treasure them in my heart.

COME UP HERE

November 20

"Then they heard a loud voice from heaven say to them, 'Come up here.' So they went up to heaven in a cloud as their enemies looked on." Revelations 11:12

In my vision I saw a ladder leading into heaven. There were angels coming and going on the ladder. Jesus said to me, "My child, one day you too will go up into heaven with the angels. They will help you climb up to heaven. They will guide you and protect you from falling. They will show you the way. There will be rejoicing in heaven with music to welcome you into my kingdom. You will see all your loved ones waiting for you. They will welcome you with open arms. On that day, I will make your joy complete. Come my beloved, come."

I look forward to the day when I can see you face to face, Lord. My guardian angel, please guide me and protect me on the way to heaven.

BURDEN AND SIN

November 21

"Since we are surrounded by so great a cloud of witnesses, let us rid ourselves of every burden and sin that clings to us and persevere in running the race that lies before us while keeping our eyes fixed on Jesus, the leader and perfecter of faith." Hebrews 12:1-2

In my vision I saw myself running in my running clothes, with people sitting all around the track. They were watching me and cheering me on. I was getting tired from running, but when I saw Jesus in front of me encouraging me on, I felt renewed energy to continue my race. Jesus said to me, "My child, have courage. Do not give up the race. Try to get rid of anything that is still a burden on your shoulders. In order to win the race you must carry nothing that will weigh you down, such as worries, anxieties and sins. Get rid of all those thoughts that will distract you from reaching your goal. Worry and anxiety are useless. Instead, focus upon me. See the spiritual world around you and know that I am with you."

Thank you, Jesus, for encouraging me. Now I understand why we must empty ourselves when we follow you. Help me to be focused only on you.

GO HOME

November 22

"Go home to your family and announce to them all that the Lord in his pity has done for you." Mark 5:19

My precious child, not everyone is called to be a missionary. For some people it is better to stay home and minister to those in need right in their own home and neighborhood. This man, who had an unclean spirit, can do more good by spreading the good news in his own town, because the people there begged me to leave after their pigs were drowned in the ocean. They were upset with me because they did not want to change their livelihood. Raising pigs was their career. They put money above everything else. Their hearts were not ready to receive my love. As for you, my child, you can also minister to others right in your own neighborhood. You do not need to go far. There is much work to be done right where you live. Go home and spread the good news to all you meet. I will be with you.

Yes Lord, there is a lot of work to be done right here where I live. Please give me the courage to share your good news with others around me. Never let me miss a chance to proclaim how great you are.

HOSPITALITY

November 23

"Do not neglect hospitality, for through it some have unknowingly entertained angels." Hebrews 13:2

In my vision I saw Abraham sitting under a large shaded tree with three men who were angels. Jesus said to me, "My child, whenever you are hospitable and kind to others, God will send angels to visit you and to bring good tidings to you. The angels told Abraham that Sarah would be pregnant by the following year even though she was beyond child-bearing age. Nothing is impossible with God. The gift of hospitality brings love and joy into your home. Whatever you do to others, you will be rewarded a hundred-fold. The measure that you measure for others will be measured to you. Be generous, be loving and kind. You will never lack for anything when you are generous with others."

Thank you, Lord, for this beautiful lesson. You have taught me to be more hospitable and generous with others, especially those less fortunate than I.

I THANK HIM

November 24

"He saved me from evil of every kind and preserved me in time of trouble. For this reason I thank him and I praise him; I bless the name of the Lord." Sirach 51:12

In my vision I saw a multitude of people kneeling in front of the Almighty God, praising and worshiping him. Jesus said to me, "It is the greatest joy when my people give us thanks and praises. For we know that it can come only from the heart. My child, give honor and glory to my Father always, for he deserves all your praises. He has glorified me and now you can do the same for him. His love for you is everlasting. Through praise and thanksgiving you will receive joy- a joy that is not from this world but from me. This is a joy that is so profound and deep that no one or circumstance can change it. This joy can sustain you and carry you through all the trials and tribulations of this world. Give thanks always."

I thank you and praise you, my Lord and my God. I am forever grateful for all you have given me. You are an awesome God.

TOUCH

November 25

"Whatever villages or towns or countryside Jesus entered, they laid the sick in the market places and begged him that they might touch only the tassel on his cloak; and as many as touched it were healed." Mark 6: 56

My loving child, it takes faith to believe that even my garment can heal. With faith everything is possible. Just believe in me. In fact, you do not even have to touch me to be healed. Just hearing my word will heal you too. The ten lepers asked me to heal them. All ten were healed even though I did not touch anyone of them. I only told them to go and see a priest. My word has as much power as the tassel on my cloak. He who believes in me will not only be healed but will live forever. My child, come and sit by me often and listen to my voice. You will be healed not only physically but also spiritually and emotionally. You will be touched by my presence and my love. My love for you will heal all your ills. Do you believe in me, my child?

Yes, Lord, I do believe. I know you are the Almighty God who created the entire universe. Nothing is impossible for you. Lord, please heal me.

WOMAN

November 26

"This one, at last, is bone of my bones and flesh of my flesh; this one shall be called 'woman'." Genesis 2:23

My beloved, you are bone of my bones and flesh of my flesh. Every time you receive my body and drink my blood we become one. We are united in mind, body and spirit. You are my spouse. That is why I have prepared a wedding banquet to receive you when you come into my kingdom. You are my precious one and I have loved you from the day you were conceived in your mother's womb. You are mine. Everyone who receives my body and my blood will have eternal life with me in heaven. That is why I had to leave my Father and come into the world so that I could come and bring you home. You are the joy of my heart. Nothing can separate me from you except sin. The wage of sin is death. And I have conquered death on the cross for you. Come, my love.

Lord Jesus, I give you my heart, body and soul. I am yours. Take me and let me never let me go.

THREE DAYS

November 27

"My heart is moved with pity for the crowd, because they have been with me now for three days and have nothing to eat." Mark 8:2

In my vision I saw Jesus sitting on a large rock and talking. He was teaching a crowd of a few thousand people in front of him. They were all engrossed in his teaching. They had a thirst for his words of wisdom. Even though they looked tired and hungry after three days, they did not want to leave Jesus. Jesus said to me, "My child, anyone who spends time listening to me will not go away empty-handed. These people who spent three days with me saw the miracle of loaves and fishes. I nourished them not only physically but also emotionally and spiritually. I gave each one of them hope and revealed to them the love of my Father. I told them how special each one of them was. That is why they did not want to go home. When you spend three days with me, such as a retreat weekend, you too will be fed and nourished. You will be enriched beyond your expectation. I will never send you away hungry."

Thank you, Jesus, for nourishing me during my last retreat. It was a faith-filled weekend.

BE RECONCILED

November 28

"Therefore, if you bring your gift to the altar, and there recall that your brother has anything against you, leave your gift there at the altar, go first and be reconciled with your brother, and then come and offer your gift." Matthew 5:23-24

My precious child, when there is someone who has a grudge or anger against you it will affect your well being. Do not delay speaking to the person who has anything against you. If you are in the right, you need to clarify the situation with that person in a loving way. If you have stepped on his toes by mistake, you need to apologize. Do not let anything come between you and others. Let every relationship be reconciled. Ask forgiveness even when you know the other person has hurt you. There must be some reason for this person to have offended you. Be the first one to reconcile with him. Be humble and admit the wrong you have done. Have a forgiving heart always. Only through forgiveness will you be able to love others as I love you.

My Jesus, you love every person in this world, even your enemies who wanted to kill you. Teach me how to love others, especially those who are difficult for me to love.

SEEK HIM

November 29

"But without faith it is impossible to please him, for anyone who approaches God must believe that he exists and that he rewards those who seek him." Hebrews 11:6

In my vision I saw myself in a dark room looking for something. But I could not see anything until I picked up a flashlight. When I turned it on, I could see what I was seeking. Jesus said to me, "I am the light of the world. You will be able to find God only when you have my light. Without me, you will fumble in the dark. You will trip and fall. With me, you can see clearly where you are going. As long as you hold on to me, you will be walking in the right path. Have faith in me; nothing else matters. Faith will lead you to my Father who loves you as much as I love you. My Father and I are one. Whoever knows me knows my Father. The Holy Spirit will reveal all truth to you."

Father, Son and Holy Spirit, I love you and I adore you. Jesus, I seek you and I long for you with my whole heart.

FISHERS OF MEN

November 30

"Come after me, and I will make you fishers of men." Matthew 4:19

My precious disciple, to catch a fish, you need to use a juicy worm or a piece of insect to entice it. To be a fisher of men, you need to speak my word and be permeated with my love in order to entice them. Arguments and lectures do not bring souls closer to me. They will only turn people away. But words of comfort and wisdom will bring love and joy into their hearts. Only then will they experience my presence and my love. Bring my heart along with you when you go out fishing for men. Put on love above all. Without love and patience, your work will be like an empty gong. Go and enjoy fishing!

Thank you, Lord, for this revelation. Fill my heart with your love every time I go out to be a fisher of men. It is a joy to be your disciple.

SEVEN BASKETS FULL

December 1

"They all ate and were satisfied. They picked up the fragments leftover – seven baskets full." Matthew 15:37

My precious child, my heart was moved to compassion for the crowd. It was my desire to provide all their needs and beyond. This crowd came to the deserted place to listen to my words. They had faith in me. They brought the sick and I cured them all. They rejoiced and glorified me. Their lives were never the same after this event. Every time you go to church to attend Mass, the same happens. Bring the sick people to the church and I will heal them and feed them with my body and my blood. Their lives will be transformed. They will never go home hungry. I am a God who loves to feed my people. I will never send you home empty handed.

Lord, give me the boldness to bring others to the church so that you might feed them and heal them. You are the most generous and compassionate God.

LORD

December 2

"Why do you call me, 'Lord, Lord,' but not do what I command?" Luke 6:46

In my vision I saw two trees. One had lots of leaves and fruit with deep roots into the ground and the other tree was small with only a few leaves on the branches. When a flood came, the second tree was washed away with the flood water while the first tree remained standing. Jesus said to me, "My child, only those who are rooted in me are the good trees that will remain standing when the trials come. Everyone who calls me, 'Lord, Lord' but does nothing and continues to live each day without me, will fall and perish. My child, you who listen to my words daily and act upon them will bear much fruit. When life gets difficult, your faith will save you. For you love me deeply. You will stand firm and will not fall."

Lord Jesus, your words are everlasting. Teach me to be ready to act upon them every day of my life.

DO YOU BELIEVE

December 3

"When he entered the house, the blind men approached him and Jesus said to them, 'Do you believe that I can do this?' 'Yes, Lord,' they said to him." Matthew 9:28

My loving child, do you believe that I can heal you? Do you truly believe that I am a healer? Have no doubt in your heart when you ask me for anything. When you doubt my ability to heal you or others, you are blocking my healing power to flow through you or to others. With faith and trust in me, all things are possible. If you can visualize it, it will come true. Name one incident in the scripture where I have turned people away when they asked for healing. There is none. Everyone who came to me was healed. So come with expectant faith in your heart. Come and I will heal you, my child.

You are my almighty God and healer. I believe that everything is possible with you.

MY PEACE

December 4

"Peace I leave you; my peace I give to you. Not as the world gives do I give it to you." John 14:27

In my vision I saw myself embraced by Jesus. He had his arms around me and I placed my head upon his shoulder. I felt so peaceful and so loved. Jesus said to me, "My precious child, when you are loved by me all your fears and anxieties will vanish. Because you know without a doubt that I will protect you from all harm. Like a baby in a mother's arms, you will feel complete security and love. You will feel content. Even though chaos might be all around you in my arms you will feel peaceful. You know that I will carry you to safety. There is nothing to fear. Even in the midst of trial, there I will be with you. You can count on me. I will never abandon you or forsake you. You are mine."

My Jesus, I love you and I place my trust in you. Fill my heart with your peace. Let me never be separated from your embrace.

ONE VOICE

December 5

"May the God of endurance and encouragement grant you to think in harmony with one another, in keeping with Christ Jesus, that with one accord you may with one voice glorify the God and Father of our Lord Jesus Christ." Romans 15:5-6

My loving child, when you pray together with a group of people as during a church service, it is most pleasing to me and to my Father. For I love to see my children united in prayer with their hearts in harmony with each other. It is a very effective way to pray. Your prayers will be brought to my Father's throne by the angels and he will reward you and answer all your petitions. When you pray together, it is like a symphony with many different instruments playing together making beautiful music. So it is when you pray with many people. It is like music to my ears. Continue to praise and worship me and my Father daily.

Glory, glory, glory in the highest! May my Lord be praised and honored forever.

JOY AND GLADNESS

December 6

"Those whom the Lord has ransomed will return and enter Zion singing, crowned with everlasting joy; they will meet with joy and gladness, sorrow and mourning will flee." Isaiah 35:10

Do you remember the time you spent alone with your mother making a project together? You enjoyed each other's company so much. You knew in your heart that you were the apple of her eye. That is what the everlasting joy will be when you spend eternity with me in heaven. You will have the same feeling of contentment just knowing how much you are loved. My presence will bring you such joy. But you do not have to wait long to receive this joy. You can have it now if you invite me into your home and into your heart. My presence will bring you joy and gladness that will overflow to others. So, my dear child, do open your heart to receive me during this Advent.

My home and my heart are open to receive you, my Lord. Come and be with me during this Advent.

MY JOY

December 7

"I have told you this so that my joy might be in you and your joy might be complete." John 15:11

In my vision I saw a couple honeymooning sitting on a beach in each other's arms enjoying the sunset together. What a beautiful and joyful picture! Jesus said to me, "My beloved, when you remain in my love you will have my joy in your heart. Perfect love casts out all fear. Everything you do, you will do it willingly for me. You will keep your soul pure just as these newlyweds. All the bride wants is to please her husband. And all the groom wants is to make his bride happy. There is no sacrifice too great for them because they are so in love with each other. Their joy is complete in each other's arms. Their hearts beat as one. They feel so content with each other. That is the kind of union that I long to have with you. Come, my love. Come, into my arms. Receive my joy and your joy will be complete."

I love you, Lord. I adore you and I worship you. You are my joy!

FAVORED ONE

December 8

"Hail, favored one! The Lord is with you." Luke 1:28

My mother Mary was full of grace. But you, my child, are blessed and filled with my grace too. For you are also chosen to do God's will. Every time you say "yes" to me, you are imitating my mother. Every time you hold my people tenderly in your arms, you love them as my mother loves me. She is your model. She sacrificed her own plans and dreams in order to carry out my will. She was the most obedient servant to my Father. She was willing to lay down her life for me. When she said "yes" to angel Gabriel, she could have been stoned to death because of her pregnancy before her marriage to Joseph, who was planning to put her away quietly. She suffered greatly seeing her only child crucified on the cross. Imitate her courage and obedience to God.

Hail Mary, Mother of God, teach me to love Jesus as much as you did. Pray for me now and at the hour of my death. Amen.

FEAR NOT

December 9

"I am the Lord, your God, who grasps your right hand; it is I who say to you, 'Fear not, I will help you.'" Isaiah 41:13

In my vision I saw my father holding my hand when I was a little child, crossing the street. He made sure that I was protected from all cars. God the Father said to me, "My precious child, do hold on to my hand. Do not walk before me or behind me. Stay close to me. Walk by my side always. Call on me and hold on to me. With me at your side, you have nothing to fear, for I am your Father and your protector. I will shelter you from all the evil ones. I will be your shield and your wall of protection. You can trust in me."

Almighty God, you are truly my loving and caring Father. I praise you and worship you forever.

YOUR REDEEMER

December 10

"Thus says the Lord, your redeemer, the Holy One of Israel: I the Lord, your God, teach you what is for your good, and lead you on the way you should go." Isaiah 48:17

In my vision I saw Jesus on the cross with his right hand reaching down to hold my hand. He said to me, "My child, I have paid the price to set you free from your sins and from this world. Even though you are living in this world you belong to me. Your time here on earth is very short compared to eternity. So spend each day holding on to my hand and never let me go. I will guide you and lead you to the right path. With your free hand, you can hold on to others and bring them to me. For I thirst for each soul. I have suffered and died for each one of them too. I want everyone to be redeemed. It is my will and my deepest desire."

Lord, hold me tight and never let me go. I want to be with you always together with your Father and the Holy Spirit. Thank you for redeeming me.

ETERNAL LIFE

December 11

"Now this is eternal life, that they should know you, the only true God, and the one whom you sent, Jesus Christ." John 17:3

My loving child, when you are in love it seems like time stands still. So it is when you know my Father and see him face to face. You will enjoy life for eternity with us. You will have peace and joy that you have never experienced on earth. Your heart will sing and you will have tears of joy. You will be overflowing with God's love. You will live forever in the presence of the almighty God, who is your Father. You will be in my arms and surrounded by all those who love you. There will be angels and saints all around you to welcome you and to love you. You will see smiling faces everywhere you go. You will hear angelic music and see beautiful scenery. You will be with us forever.

Wow! I can hardly wait for that day when I will be with you for eternity, my Lord and my God.

YOU WILL RECEIVE

December 12

"Until now you have not asked anything in my name; ask and you will receive, so that your joy may be complete." John 16:24

Do you remember when you were a teenager and asked your mother for a special Christmas present? Even though your mother did not think that you should have it, she knew how much you wanted it and she gave you exactly what you asked for Christmas. Remember how happy you were when you received your present? You knew how much your mother loved you and that she would never refuse you anything you asked from her. My Father in heaven loves you with an infinite love. Do you think he will refuse you anything? I know he will give you anything when you ask in my name. He loves you as much as I love you. He wants you to have joy that no human being can give you. You are his precious child and he loves to give you gifts.

My heavenly Father, thank you for loving me so much. You have always answered my prayers.

A STAR

December 13

"A star shall advance from Jacob, and a staff shall rise from Israel." Numbers 24:17

My child, it was predicted years ago that I would send my only Son into the world to save you. Jesus came into the world to show you how to live with love in your heart. He came to teach you that with love you will be able to conquer all evil. Jesus is the way, the truth and the life. Whoever follows my Son will have eternal life, because he alone knows the way to my heart. He came into the world to do my will. His love for me is so great that he was willing to sacrifice his life for you. Every time you see a star in the sky, remember how much we love you and how special you are to us.

Loving Father, thank you for sending your only Son, Jesus, into my life. I love you both with my whole heart.

CONQUERED THE WORLD

December 14

"In the world you will have trouble, but take courage, I have conquered the world." John 16:33

In my vision I saw a wall dividing two sides. One side was filled with light and the other side was in darkness. Jesus crumbled the wall into pieces and the darkness on one side disappeared. Jesus said to me, "The bright side is my kingdom and the dark side is the evil world. I have conquered the world. The wall has fallen. Are you willing to pick up the pieces of the wall that separated the two sides for me and build my kingdom with them? Will you be my hands and my feet in this world? It is hard labor but your reward will be great. With the broken pieces you can pave the road and lead others to me. My apostles all were willing to pave the road with their martyrdom. Are you willing to lay down your life for me too? Come and follow me."

My Jesus, with your help I will be able to follow you. Please help me to overcome all fear and anxiety so that I will be able to do your will.

TURN TO ME

December 15

"Turn to me and be safe, all you ends of the earth, for I am God, there is no other!" Isaiah 45:22

In my vision I saw a field of yellow sunflowers all facing the sun. Jesus said to me, "When you are with me, I will protect you from all harm. When you are far away from me, you will stumble and fall. Turn yourself around like the sunflowers and face me as soon as you are feeling depressed or lonely. Do not be tempted to remain in darkness. Walk towards the light, for I am the light of the world. I will show you the way and lead you in the right path. It is a choice you make each day. You can come and follow me or you can do your own will. You can worship me or you can be self sufficient and have no need of my help. When that happens, your pride will take over and you will fall. So turn to me and be safe."

I will follow you always, my Lord. You are my one and only God and Savior.

HUSBAND

December 16

"For he who has become your husband is your Maker, his name is the Lord of hosts; your redeemer is the Holy One of Israel, called God of all the earth." Isaiah 54:5

My love, I will always cherish you. I long to hold you in my embrace. But you are always busy with so many things. Like your grandchild moving the toys from one room to another. Never sitting still. Always active. My joy is when you sit quietly with me. Like two lovers holding hands. Not saying any words to each other, but with the joy of knowing that you are mine. We share the same goal in life. We share our deepest thoughts and we love to listen to each other's voice. I love you with an everlasting love. I will never leave you. You are my spouse.

Praise to you, my loving Father, Son and Holy Spirit. It is a joy to know that you are my spouse and the love of my life. My cup overflows.

HEARTS BE TROUBLED

December 17

"Do not let your hearts be troubled. You have faith in God; have faith also in me." John 14:1

In my vision I saw a child playing joyfully in the playground. He was not worried about anything, because he knew that his parents were close by and watching after him. His only focus was to have a good time. Jesus said to me, "My precious child, can you see how happy the little child in your vision was? Only because he knew that he had nothing to fear with his parents nearby protecting him. I am watching you every moment of your life, whether you are working, resting or eating. My eyes are always upon you. Feel my presence, my child. You have nothing to fear. I will be with you every minute of your life. Take a deep breath and visualize me standing right next to you. Have faith in me."

In the name of Jesus Christ and by the power of the Holy Spirit I call on the spirit of fear to leave me right now and to go to the foot of the cross and never to come back to harass me. Thank you, Jesus.

JESUS

December 18

"She will bear a son and you are to name him Jesus, because he will save his people from their sins." Matthew 1:21

My loving child, if you know how precious each soul is to my Father, you will know why he sent me into this world to die on the cross for you. Each sin is like a dagger piercing my heart. Each sin inflicts a wound on my flesh. Each sin nails me to the cross. Each sin whips my back until my flesh comes off my body. Each sin jabs a thorn into my head. But I suffer willingly for you, my child. My Father and I want you to spend eternity with us in heaven. We want you to be a part of our Family. We want you to enjoy the banquet with us forever. Go and sin no more.

Jesus, thank you for saving me from my sinful ways. I love you more than anyone else in this world. Your name is like music in my ears and I want to praise you always.

EMMANUEL

December 19

"Behold, the virgin shall conceive and bear a son, and they shall name him Emmanuel, which means 'God is with us.'" Matthew 1:23

My child, do you feel my presence at all times during the day? Know without a doubt that I am with you always. I will never leave you or forsake you. You are my flesh and blood. Do you know when you receive me during the Eucharist your body is transformed and united with mine? We are one. We cannot be separated, except by sin. For the wage of sin is death. I am life. Whoever comes to me will have abundant life, a life filled with love and joy. You will receive the power of the Holy Spirit like Mary, my mother. For where I am, there is also my loving Father. We are three persons in one God. We are inseparable like you and me. We are forever together.

Come Emmanuel. Come, Holy Spirit. Come, my loving Father. Come into my heart and stay with me forever. Never let me be separated from you, O Holy Trinity.

FAVOR WITH GOD

December 20

"Then the angel said to her, 'Do not be afraid, Mary, for you have found favor with God.'" Luke 1:30

Do not be afraid, my child, for you also have found favor with God. You too are my precious spouse and I have chosen you. You have a special mission to do that only you can fulfill for me. Your existence in this world is unique. It cannot be duplicated by another person. Your personality and temperament are perfect for the job that I have planned for you. No one has the same assignment as you. When you answered "yes" to me, I provided you with courage and strength to carry out all that I have planned for you to do. Thank you for being willing to do my will. Thank you for opening your mind and your heart to receive me. Thank you for being my special servant and friend. I love you always.

Lord, I am your handmaid and your servant. Let it be done according to your will.

THE INFANT LEAPED

December 21

"When Elizabeth heard Mary's greetings, the infant leaped in her womb, and Elizabeth filled with the Holy Spirit, cried out in a loud voice and said, 'Most blessed are you among women, and blessed is the fruit of your womb.'" Luke 1:41-42

My precious child, you are just as blessed as my mother Mary. For you also carry me inside your heart. Every time you receive communion, you receive me: body, blood, soul and divinity. You carry me everywhere you go. Bring joy to all you meet as my mother did. Mary went to help her cousin Elizabeth right after she heard the good news from Angel Gabriel. She was there to help with all the household chores and stayed with Elizabeth until John the Baptist was born. She was there to help deliver the baby and wash his diapers. She brought joy to the entire household. Be like my mother Mary.

Lord, I love to bring your joy to others. Give me the strength to carry out all that you want me to do for you. Mary, my mother, pray for me.

MY SPIRIT REJOICES

December 22

"My soul proclaims the greatness of the Lord; my spirit rejoices in God my Savior, for he has looked upon his handmaid's lowliness; behold, from now on will all ages call me blessed." Luke 1:46-48

Joy is one of the fruits of the Holy Spirit. My mother was filled with the Holy Spirit when she heard that she would be the mother of God. You too were filled with my Spirit at baptism. In a few days Christmas will be here. Prepare to receive me as my mother did. Make room in your heart for me. Place me in the center of your life and never let me go. Invite me to stay with you always. Share with me all your joys and sorrows. I want to be with you every moment of your life. I long to be loved by you and by everyone. You are my precious child and I have redeemed you with my blood on the cross. You are mine. Rejoice and be glad. Know that you belong to me.

Come to me, my Jesus. My heart is joyful and eager to receive you into my heart.

REFINER'S FIRE

December 23

"For he is like the refiner's fire, or like the fuller's lye. He will sit refining and purifying silver, and he will purify the sons of Levi, refining them like gold or like silver that they may offer due sacrifice to the Lord." Malachi 3:2-3

In my vision I saw a man working. He was beating metal with his hammer and he tried to shape it in the furnace to mold it into a heart shape. Jesus said to me, "My precious child, you are being refined every day. When you are ready to give up your own agenda totally for my sake that is when your heart will turn into gold, so pure that I will be able to see myself in your heart. Only then will people be able to see me in you. Only then, people will know me through you. They will no longer see you but me. I am a skillful refiner and will not harm or hurt you. I am gentle and patient with you. You have nothing to fear. When your heart finally becomes like mine, you will shine like the morning sun. You will rejoice in my love."

Lord, transform me into your image and likeness. I want to do your will always. You are more precious to me than gold and silver.

OUR SALVATION

December 24

"He has raised up for us a horn for our salvation within the house of David his servant." Luke 1:69

My loving child, I have sent my only Son into the world to show you what true love is. Jesus has a heart full of compassion and mercy. He loves you and everyone with my perfect love. His heart goes out to anyone who cries out to me. He came to save you. His love is a sacrificial love; he lays down his life for you. There is no greater love than his. Can you imagine yourself giving your own son to die on the cross for others? Can you? This Christmas, my loving child, let your heart be filled with my love so that you can reflect Jesus' love to all. Especially those who need his love the most.

Alleluia! Blessed is he who comes in the name of the Lord! Hosanna in the highest!

RADIANT

December 25

"Then you shall be radiant at what you see, your heart shall throb and overflow, for the riches of the sea shall be emptied before you, the wealth of nations shall be brought to you." Isaiah 60:5

My child, I am the light of the world. When you come close to me you will receive radiant light. Your face will glow with delight because you will see all the miracles and wonders that only I can do. You will rejoice and your heart will overflow with awe. You will see my glory as you come ever closer to me. You will know how much I really love you and care about you. Your face will shine like a person who is in love. Your heart will leap with joy and your steps will be quickened with hope. There is nothing that I will not give you. All the treasures are for you to take for I am your Christ.

Christ Jesus, my Lord and my God. I worship you and I adore you. You are my King of Kings and Lord of Lords.

MUST BE PREPARED

December 26

"So too, you also must be prepared, for an hour you do not expect, the Son of Man will come." Matthew 24:44

In my vision I saw people getting ready for a big storm to arrive at their town. They were boarding up their glass windows, buying plenty of water and food to last a few days and putting the house in order so that there would be the least amount of damage. Jesus said to me, "So it is with you. Be prepared for my coming when you least expect. Put on the armor of God daily, read the scriptures and store up my words in your heart. Receive my body and my blood so I will be able to strengthen you during trials. Go to confession often and prepare your soul to meet me when I come. Pray constantly in the spirit. Do good while you still have the time. The days are growing shorter and shorter. Do not sit around idle watching TV for hours. Every minute is precious. My child, when I come, be ready to receive me. I am coming soon."

Prepare my heart and my soul to receive you, O Lord. I look forward to your coming.

WITNESS

December 27

"I earnestly bore witness for both Jews and Greeks to repentance before God and to faith in our Lord Jesus." Acts 20:21

My loving child, to be a witness is to tell others about your own experiences with me. There is no greater message than to tell others what I have done for you. People will believe you when they see the smile on your face. They will know that I have transformed your life. I have given you grace after grace. You will be like Stephen, whose face became like an angel before he was stoned to death. He saw heaven opened and he was not afraid to die. So it is with you, when you feel my presence and know how much I love you, you will glow with joy and you will want to tell everyone about me. Be my witness at all times to anyone who is open to hear the good news. It will transform their lives. It will increase their faith in me.

Lord Jesus, you have done so many miracles in my life. I will tell others how great you are. I will go and be your witness.

THE LAW

December 28

"Amen, I say to you, until heaven and earth pass away, not the smallest letter or the smallest part of a letter will pass from the law, until all things have taken place." Matthew 5:18

In my vision I saw a house built on stilts. As long as all the stilts were intact, the house was not in danger of falling into the water. But when the stilts were broken, the house crumbled and fell. Jesus said to me, "My loving child, the laws are like the stilts supporting you in everything you do. When you break one of my laws, your foundation is shaken. Only through repentance and confession will you be able to rebuild your house. I am your cornerstone. Without me you will fall. Without the laws you will perish. Your entire well-being is based on the law of love. Without love you will not be able to live an abundant life."

My Rock and my Savior, on you I will build my house. Your law is my delight and my stronghold.

THE END

December 29

"When you hear of wars and insurrections, do not be terrified; for such things must happen first, but it will not immediately be the end." Luke 21:9

In my vision I saw resurrected Jesus in a white dazzling garment coming down from heaven. Jesus said to me, "My child, I am your hope and your salvation. No matter how bad the situation on earth is, you have nothing to fear. I will be with you until the end of times. I will protect you from all harm. I will not leave you or forsake you. For you are precious in my sight. I will come and bring you to my Father. The Holy Spirit will give you the wisdom and knowledge to know the truth and to follow me in times of peril. You will have the courage to go through all trials. Have no fear in your heart. Nothing will touch you unless it is permitted by me. I will never leave you. You are my beloved child."

My Jesus, I long for the day when I will see you face to face. You are my Savior and my Redeemer. In you I trust.

LOVES THE WORLD

December 30

"If anyone loves the world, the love of the Father is not in him. For all that is in the world, sensual lust, enticement for the eyes, and a pretentious life, is not from the Father but is from the world." 1 John 2:15-16

In my vision I saw a Ferris wheel in a fairground all lighted up that went round and round. Jesus said to me, "My child, when you enjoy worldly things, it is like riding on a Ferris wheel. It goes nowhere except round and round. But when you put me first in your life, you are climbing a ladder up into heaven. You will be guided by my angels on both sides of the ladder like the angels Jacob saw in his dream. Seek me and climb the ladder. Sometimes climbing seems difficult compared to riding the Ferris wheel. But the ladder will lead you to heaven while the Ferris wheel leads you to nowhere. It has no purpose except to give you temporary pleasure while you are riding on it. Choose me. Choose the narrow way."

Thank you, Lord, for your words of wisdom. I will climb the ladder with your help. Strengthen me and lead me to your heart.

YEAR OF JUBILEE

December 31

"In the fiftieth year, your year of jubilee, you shall not sow, nor shall you reap the after-growth or pick the grapes from the untrimmed vines." Leviticus 25:11

In my vision I saw trumpets being played and people celebrating and rejoicing. Jesus said to me, "My loving child, it is good to stop and celebrate the milestones in your life. You need to recognize all the blessings that I have showered over you in the previous year. Let all past wrongdoings be wiped away with my precious blood. Let your life start with a clean slate. Rejoice and be glad. This is the year of jubilee for you, for I have redeemed you and forgiven all your past sins. All your family will be blessed because of you. You will return to me and I will shower you with my love and forgiveness. Let there be no more tears and shame. This is the year for you to rejoice in the Lord."

Rejoice and be glad! Thank you, Lord, for giving me this special year of grace. Fill me with your hope and love.

CPSIA information can be obtained
at www.ICGtesting.com
Printed in the USA
BVOW08s1703040418
512450BV00018B/465/P

9 781593 308339